I0112055

HOSEA

Faithful God, Unfaithful People

Richard Caldwell

KRESS BIBLICAL RESOURCES

Copyright © 2019 Richard Caldwell

All rights reserved.

Published by:
Kress Biblical Resources
www.kressbiblical.com

Unless otherwise indicated, all scripture quotations are from the ESV® Bible (The Holy Bible, English Standard Version®), copyright © 2001 by Crossway, a publishing ministry of Good News Publishers. Used by permission. All rights reserved.

NASB: Scripture quotations taken from the New American Standard Bible® (NASB), Copyright © 1960, 1962, 1963, 1968, 1971, 1972, 1973,1975, 1977, 1995 by The Lockman Foundation. Used by permission. www.Lockman.org

NIV: Scripture taken from the Holy Bible, NEW INTERNATIONAL VERSION®, NIV® Copyright © 1973, 1978, 1984, 2011 by Biblica, Inc.® Used by permission. All rights reserved worldwide.

NET Bible: Scripture quoted by permission. Quotations designated (NET) are from the NET Bible® copyright ©1996-2016 by Biblical Studies Press, L.L.C. http://netbible.com All rights reserved.

ISBN: 978-1-934952-52-8

DEDICATION

To the congregation at Founders Baptist Church. Their kindness and love to me and my family has allowed me to devote myself to study and preaching with joy.

CONTENTS

1
A Living Sermon
(1:1-2:1)

Hosea is the longest of the 12 Minor Prophets. They are not called minor because their message is less important, but because they are shorter works. It stands at the head of the Minor Prophets, and so it should, not only because of its length, but also because of its powerful message. No prophet had a more unique calling than the prophet Hosea. God chose him to be a living object lesson for the message he was to preach. He and his family would be a picture of the relationship between the Lord and His people. James Montgomery Boice refers to Hosea as the second greatest story ever told,[1] after the story of Christ Himself.

God chose him to be a living object lesson for the message he was to preach. Hosea would model God's relationship to His people, and his wife would treat Hosea the way that God's people treated God. His children would picture the individual Israelites and God's attitudes toward them.

Hosea is the last prophet to the northern kingdom, Israel, just prior to the invasion and destruction brought about by the Assyrians in 722 B.C. This book has been referred by one writer as the prophet at the zero hour in Israel's history, a final warning from God concerning their judgment. While Hosea focuses most of his message on the northern kingdom, God also uses his messages as a warning trumpet to the southern kingdom. This is why you find messages concerning Judah interspersed throughout the book.

---

[1] James Montgomery Boice, *The Minor Prophets* (Grand Rapids: Kregel, 1996)

Hosea ministers for nearly 40 years. His ministry spans the rule of several kings, both in the North and the South.[2] God tells him that he will preach and experience this message of judgment and hope in the most personal way possible, in his own family and marriage.

The first section of the book consists of chapters 1-3. They serve as a prologue, as well as a miniature summary of it. The three chapters have a definite organization. Hosea's story is told in two parts. The first points to judgment, the second points to hope. Between the two narratives are three oracles. The first is an oracle of judgment; the next two are oracles of hope.

GOD'S INSTRUCTION TO HOSEA (1:1-2)

The Prophet

We really know nothing about Hosea other than what we find in this book. We know he is from the northern kingdom (7:5), that his father was named Beeri. Concerning his ministry, we know the time period—he followed the ministry of Amos. We know the length of his ministry and the content of this prophecy.

<u>The Word to the Prophet</u>

Verse 2 begins, *When the Lord first spoke through Hosea.* The Lord is speaking not only **to** Hosea, but **through** him. Next, He says, *Go, take to yourself a wife of whoredom and have children of whoredom.* What exactly did Hosea do? People have interpreted this in three ways.

OPTION ONE — In reality, he did nothing. All of this is symbolism, allegorical. He never really had a wife of whoredom and children of whoredom. But nothing in this narrative indicates that. In fact, there are details in this narrative that are completely unnecessary unless this is presenting us with historical reality. For example, we are given the name of Gomer's father.

OPTION TWO — He married someone who was already a prostitute. One of the great sins confronted in this book is the worship of Baal.

---

[2] He ministered during the reigns of four kings of Judah (the southern kingdom) and one king of Israel (the northern kingdom). Hosea in Israel would have been a contemporary of Isaiah and Micah in Judah. Some have asked why, as a prophet to the north, he lists the kings of the south. Maybe it's a way of saying that only the descendants of David (kings of Judah) were legitimate.

One aspect of Baal worship was the belief that he was the god of fertility, and one of the ways that they thought to stir the Baals to action was ritualistic sexual activity. Both males and females throughout Israel (in the lax moral condition the nation was in) participated in this. According to this view, Gomer was one of the women serving Baal in this way. They also take the words *children of whoredom* to mean that the children had the character of their mother, they see these children as already existing when Hosea marries her.

There are some major problems with this view. One, you have God commanding the prophet to marry a woman who is already living in sexual sin. Two, it would really destroy the comparison that will be made throughout this book. Israel had a good beginning because she was married to a faithful husband, but she then proved to be unfaithful to him.

OPTION THREE — Hosea marries a woman, having been told in advance that she will not be faithful to him. That is, he marries an Israelite woman who is not a prostitute. They have a good beginning, but then she becomes unfaithful to him.

This, I believe, is the right view to take on this command. In addition, the words *children of whoredom* I take to mean something different than the statement about the wife. These children are the offspring of whoredom. Hosea will come face to face with the sad situation of his wife bearing children that are not his.

The Significance of the Command

This is a picture of the behavior of his people. Hosea will be a living letter to the nation of Israel. They will see that he knows something of the pain of Yahweh, because he is living through this same kind of pain himself, although to a much lesser degree. God's people have become spiritual adulteresses and represent children of whoredom. This book puts a focus on the false religion of Baal, and Israel's pursuit of it.

HOSEA'S OBEDIENCE TO GOD (1:3A)

He immediately obeys the Lord by taking Gomer[3] to be his wife. The prophet may not fully understand what he is about to live through, but whatever this word will mean for him, his response is one of immediate obedience to God.

HOSEA'S SIGNIFICANT FAMILY (1:3-9)

The Son Named Jezreel (1:4)

Hosea is to name his son Jezreel, because the Lord will soon *punish the house of Jehu for the blood of Jezreel*. The Valley of Jezreel is the place where Ahab and Jezebel had Naboth, an innocent man, put to death so that they could take his vineyard. It is also the place where Jehu began his slaughter of Joram and the entire house of Ahab. It seems strange that Jehu's house would be punished for this. Jehu acted on the command of God through Elisha the prophet (2 Kgs 9:6-10, and he is commended by God for having done this (2 Kgs 10:30). This can be explained in a couple of ways.

OPTION ONE — In this case, the name Jehu is synonymous with Israel, and what is being avenged is the death of Naboth in connection with the vineyard. The ESV Study Bible explains this view:

Many suppose that the **blood of Jezreel** refers to the shedding of blood of the house of Ahab and Ahaziah when Jehu usurped the throne (2 Kings 9:21-28). But this proposal suffers from serious difficulties. First, the kingdom of Israel did not come to an end with Jehu's dynasty. Israel survived for 30 years after Zechariah, the last king of that dynasty. Second, God commanded Jehu to exterminate Ahab's dynasty, and commended his work (2 Kings 9:1-10; 10:30; cf. 2 Chron 22:7). It seems unlikely that the Lord would punish someone for carrying out his command. It is better to take the phrase "house of Jehu" as parallel to **house of Israel**, and thus another name for Israel. By this reading, "the blood of Jezreel" refers to 1 Kings 21: Ahab, who promoted Baalism as the national religion of Israel, plotted to murder Naboth, a man loyal to the Lord, in order to seize his vineyard in Jezreel. Appropriately, this

---

[3] Elsewhere in scripture Gomer refers to a people group. Gen. 10:2-3, 1 Chron. 1:5-6 & Ezk. 38:6.

verse sets the tenor for the rest of the book: the ongoing confrontation between Baal and the God of Israel.[4]

OPTION TWO — Even though God commended Jehu for wiping out Ahab's dynasty, he also killed a lot of other people. Maybe God is avenging that. Jehu obeyed the words of the prophet Elijah, but his real motive wasn't the glory of God. Jehu killed unnecessarily and beyond the scope of what he had been commanded to do.

What is clear is this: <u>God remembers and avenges sin</u>. In this case, He will break Israel's *bow* (her power) in the *Valley of Jezreel*. One of the features of the book of Hosea is how he deals with their geography. It is as if Hosea gives a tour of the land, reminding the people, place by place, of the evil they have done against the Lord.

In addition, there is symmetry present in God's judgments. Where they were guilty, there their guilt will be punished, and their strength will be broken. Sin must always be confronted, either by repentance or judgment.

The Daughter Named No Mercy (Lo-Ruhamah)

Here is the first sign of a problem in this marriage. There is an indication that this is not his child. Verse 3 says *she conceived and bore him a son*. However, 1:6 says *she conceived and bore a daughter*, not bore **him** a daughter. This alone does not prove that the identity of the child's father is questioned. This kind of language is used in some other places in the Old Testament for legitimate births. But there are other factors in this book that point to a message being communicated by this language. When we get to the application of these symbols, 2:4 speaks of having *no mercy* on the children *because they are children of whoredom.*

No mercy means that the natural affection that a father would have for his children is missing. The symbolic name that is given points to the fact that judgment is upon the people. Judgment will come upon the northern kingdom soon, and there will be no mercy in the judgment. But there will still be *mercy on the house of Judah* (1:7). There is still time for the southern kingdom, and God will show himself mighty on behalf of Hezekiah. They will be saved not by their military might, but *by the LORD their God.*

---

[4] <u>ESV Study Bible</u> (Wheaton, IL: Crossway, 2008), p. 1623

The Son Named Not My People (Lo-Ammi)

This one goes a step beyond, as this child is disowned. God makes plain that His relationship with Israel has reached the point of severe discipline. Their judgment will reveal their apostate condition. They are His people in terms of physical history. They are His people in terms of their future and a covenant that God has made with respect to them, but they are not His people from a spiritual point of view. Israel has forsaken the true and living God and gone after false gods. The time of mercy is past, and judgment is going to fall. And Hosea's own marriage and children are a living sermon that shows the current relationship between the living God and the northern kingdom.

GOD'S MESSAGE OF HOPE (1:10-2:1)

Yet—in spite of all of this—*the number of the children of Israel shall be like the sand of the sea.* God's commitment to His promise to Abraham stands.

Genesis 15:1 *After these things the word of the LORD came to Abram in a vision: "Fear not, Abram, I am your shield; your reward shall be very great." ² But Abram said, "O Lord GOD, what will you give me, for I continue childless, and the heir of my house is Eliezer of Damascus?" ³ And Abram said, "Behold, you have given me no offspring, and a member of my household will be my heir." ⁴ And behold, the word of the LORD came to him: "This man shall not be your heir; your very own son shall be your heir." ⁵ And he brought him outside and said, "Look toward heaven, and number the stars, if you are able to number them." Then he said to him, "So shall your offspring be."*

Genesis 22:16 *and said, "By myself I have sworn, declares the LORD, because you have done this and have not withheld your son, your only son, ¹⁷ I will surely bless you, and I will surely multiply your offspring as the stars of heaven and as the sand that is on the seashore. And your offspring shall possess the gate of his enemies, ¹⁸ and in your offspring shall all the nations of the earth be blessed, because you have obeyed my voice."*

In the future, *in the place where it was said to them, "You are not my people,"* (that is, right here in the land, where they are hearing Hosea) *it shall be said to them, "Children of the living God."* The *children of Judah and the children of Israel* will unite under *one head*, the Messiah, the Lord Jesus Christ. The *day of Jezreel* will be *great*. Incidentally, *Jezreel* means "God sows." Although God executes judgment, He still will claim them as His people. Where there has been judgment, there will be restoration. Where there has been division, there will be reunion. Where apostasy, there will be faith and faithfulness.

THE DESIRED RESPONSE FOR THE PEOPLE (2:1)

God offers hope to them, if only they will hear, receive and believe His message, proclaiming, *"You are My people...you have received mercy."* He will accomplish salvation in a physical remnant of national Israel. God promised it to Abraham, and He's sworn by Himself to do it. Israel's adultery, her judgment and her separation from her husband is not the final word, although she deserves it. God is gracious and powerful and able to perform what He has promised.

APPLYING IT

Servants

Like Hosea, we are **servants** of God, existing to tell His story. God blesses and enriches us by allowing us to reflect His glory to the world. We are just as blessed when He puts us in difficult situations, as when He puts us in pleasanter situations. We must not see this as sacrifice, but as a great blessing.

Living Letters

Like Hosea, we are **living letters**. God makes us sermons by placing each of us in situations where we don't just hear about the gospel, or aren't just intellectually instructed about it, but rather we get put in situations where we feel the gospel and get to demonstrate it. We are called to live the gospel. For example:

- God loved us before we loved Him, and we are put in situations where we must love people who don't love us.
- God loves us when we don't love Him as we should, and we are put in situations where we must love people who mistreat us.
- God sacrificed Himself, in the person of His Son, to rescue us and forgive us of our sin, and we are put in situations where we must sacrifice for the very ones who don't care about us at all.
- God patiently, persistently and stubbornly loves us, even when we are foolish and invite His punishing hand. So, we must love people in the same way, sometimes even in discipline, always holding on to them when they would let go of us.

2 Corinthians 3:1 *Are we beginning to commend ourselves again? Or do we need, as some do, letters of recommendation to you, or from you? [2] You yourselves are our letter of recommendation, written on our hearts, to be known and read by all. [3] And you show that you are a letter from Christ delivered by us, written not with ink but with the Spirit of the living God, not on tablets of stone but on tablets of human hearts.*

Whatever we experience that provides an opportunity to express the gospel, pales in comparison with what our God has experienced from us.

This is what God is doing with Hosea. He is making Hosea and his family a sign, a living letter, a sermon by example.

2
Loving Judgment
(2:2-13)

The prophet Hosea has a unique calling. He has been called to enter into a marriage, and as a result to experience a family life that will serve as a sign to the nation of Israel. Some scholars refer to him as the deathbed prophet of Israel because he is the last prophet sent to the northern kingdom before they're taken away in captivity to Assyria, before they're destroyed. He is giving the last prophetic warning that these people will receive.

Hosea's family is a significant one. His marriage to Gomer and the children she bore would, by the plan of God, serve as a prophetic picture. The prophet now declares the message of God about the nation's relationship to God, a relationship that is pictured by Hosea's own family.

The first chapter, through verse 1 of chapter 2, focuses on Hosea's family life. Now we move to oracles, messages that God gives to Israel with Hosea's family life as a living picture of what God is saying. Chapter two contains three messages—two messages of judgment and one message of hope.

We focus here on what we know for certain.

GOD WARNS OF JUDGMENT (2:2-5)

In verses 2-5, God is warning the nation of the judgment that's coming. Then, in verses 6-13, we see God's judgments detailed, step by step. All of this comes from love, from God's steadfast covenant love toward his people. Our culture has emptied the word "love" of its true meaning. To understand love, we need to look to the Word of God. When we do that, we find that love includes more than just soft words and soft attitudes. No one loves more perfectly than God, and His love includes warnings and rebukes as well as discipline and punishment.

Rebuke for the Nation

The prophet begins by urging the children (who represent individual Israelites) to *plead* with their mother (who represents the nation as a whole). The word for *plead* means to strive with, and it is repeated for emphasis. God tells the people to plead with the nation (as a whole) to recognize its sin and to turn from it. Even any individuals who are not walking in step with the rebellious nation, any who really do have faith in the Lord, the living God, are called on to point out the sin of their nation.

As Christians today, our citizenship is in heaven. Whatever our country, we can recognize how the Lord has used it. Thank God for his mercies! However, if we live in a spiritually sick society, a nation that's already seeing signs of God's judgment upon it, we must recognize our individual responsibility. We need to walk in a different way from the path of our nation, and to *rebuke* our *mother*—to call our nation to repentance.

Recognition of the Separation

Plead with your mother, plead—for she is not my wife, and I am not her husband— This is a recognition of separation, that the real problem is that they're not walking with the Lord. They are separated from God in terms of fellowship. Some have taken this as a formal expression of divorce.[5] But this is clearly not the case. In the very next verse, judgment is expressed as a possibility, not a certainty. The children are to warn their mother *lest* her husband take action against her. In fact, by the end of the chapter, it's clear that God is not finished with Israel. We see something similar in the prophecy of Isaiah, Hosea's contemporary, who ministered primarily to the southern kingdom while Hosea ministered primarily to the northern kingdom. Isaiah spoke of a divorce.

Isaiah 50:1 *Thus says the Lord:*

---

[5] Derek Kidner reported that archaeology discovered some ancient statements of marriage in the format, "She is my wife, and I am her husband." In their view, to say, "She is not my wife, and I am not her husband," was a declaration of divorce.

"Where is your mother's certificate of divorce,
with which I sent her away?
Or which of my creditors is it
to whom I have sold you?
Behold, for your iniquities you were sold,
and for your transgressions your mother was sent away.

Yet read this later passage.

Isaiah 54:5 *For your Maker is your husband,*
the LORD of hosts is his name;
and the Holy One of Israel is your Redeemer,
the God of the whole earth he is called.
6 For the LORD has called you
like a wife deserted and grieved in spirit,
like a wife of youth when she is cast off,
says your God.
7 For a brief moment I deserted you,
but with great compassion I will gather you.
8 In overflowing anger for a moment
I hid my face from you,
but with everlasting love I will have compassion on you,"
says the LORD, your Redeemer.

When we think of God's promises concerning a future millennial time of blessing for Israel, we recognize that God has not divorced Israel in a formal sense. Rather, He is saying that Israel's relationship with Him is practically like being divorced. Israel has separated herself from Him. She's not living as His wife, so He is not relating to her as a husband. She has walked away from Him and has committed adultery. The people are acting in ways that violate their covenant with God, and the result is an alienation from God (2:13). Whenever people's lives go astray spiritually, the issue is their relationship with God. We need to help them see that, because whenever they are pursuing sin, they want to bring a host of other issues into the picture—but the real issue is their relationship with God.

Repentance Directed

God, through Hosea's words to the children, now tells her what to do. She's to *put away her whoring from her face, and her adultery from between her breasts.* The words *whoring* and *adultery* are plural in the Hebrew. Why does the Lord use plural words here? Some say it's to magnify the intensity of her unfaithfulness to God. But Hosea mentions putting away her whoring and her adultery *from her face* and *from between her breasts*. He's referring to her appearance. He's describing the nation in terms of how a woman begins to live when she's living a life of adultery; advertising herself almost like a prostitute. Notice what it says in verse 13: *And I will punish her for the feast days of the Baals when she burned offerings to them <u>and adorned herself with her ring and jewelry, and went after her lovers</u>….* God is talking there about her attire, the expressions of her immoral ways. She's dressing in a way to allure her lovers. The prophet Jeremiah gives us a similar picture.

Jeremiah 4:30 *And you, O desolate one, what do you mean that you dress in scarlet, that you adorn yourself with ornaments of gold, that you enlarge your eyes with paint? In vain you beautify yourself. Your lovers despise you; they seek your life.*

So, here in Hosea 2, God is saying that you will know the nation has repented when the nation changes its behavior. This is also true individually. How do you know when someone has repented? Their behavior changes. When someone's heart is not in a good condition, it begins to be evident in the way they dress, even in the way they present themselves, sometimes even in their countenance. These verses in Hosea 2 are a figurative way of saying that the nation must repent.

Retribution Detailed (The Judgments Warned About)

God now warns of what He may do to her, to the nation of Israel. She will be…

Stripped

This can be seen as a formal judgment of immorality. A crowd is gathered to see the prostitute stripped naked. Ezekiel spoke in a similar way to the southern kingdom of Judah.

Ezekiel 16:35 *"Therefore, O prostitute, hear the word of the LORD: ³⁶ Thus says the Lord GOD, Because your lust was poured out and your nakedness uncovered in your whorings with your lovers, and with all your abominable idols, and because of the blood of your children that you gave to them, ³⁷ therefore, behold, I will gather all your lovers with whom you took pleasure, all those you loved and all those you hated. I will gather them against you from every side and will uncover your nakedness to them, that they may see all your nakedness. ³⁸ And I will judge you as women who commit adultery and shed blood are judged, and bring upon you the blood of wrath* *and jealousy. 39 And I will give you into their hands, and they shall throw down your vaulted chamber and break down your lofty places. They shall strip you of your clothes and take your beautiful jewels and leave you naked and bare. 40 They shall bring up a crowd against you, and they shall stone you and cut you to pieces with their swords. 41 And they shall burn your houses and execute judgments upon you in the sight of many women. I will make you stop playing the whore, and you shall also give payment no more.*

She's wanted to be lewd, and her lewdness will be exposed when she is judged. She may be *naked…as in the day she was born.*

Divested

She may end up *like a wilderness, like a parched land,* killed *with thirst.* The picture is one of a husband taking back everything that he had supplied for his wife. Again, there is some indication that in the ancient Middle East this was sometimes the practice when a divorce occurred. Remember that the nation of Israel is seen as being born when it leaves Egypt, and God takes her through wilderness wanderings before she enters the promised land. When she was in the desert, in the wilderness, God took care of her. He supplied food, manna from heaven. He supplied water from a rock. He provided for the nation in supernatural ways. But now, when He judges her, she will be as she was on the day when she was born. She will be in a wilderness, but he won't take care of her. She will be like a parched land, dying from thirst. He will leave her to what she can supply for herself. And she will discover she hasn't supplied anything for herself.

National Judgment (2:2-3)

This judgment has to do with the *mother,* who represents the nation as a whole. Though the people ARE the nation, there is a distinction made here for purpose of emphasis.

Individual Judgment (2:4)

2:4 *Upon her children also I will have no mercy, because they are children of whoredom.*

The impact goes all the way down to the individual level. Individual members of the nation will suffer what will generally be true for everyone. There is no escape. What God is going to do with Assyria toward the northern kingdom, will impact every single individual citizen of the nation.

The people must see themselves not just as a collective whole, but also realize the individual impact of what the nation has been doing toward the Lord.

God is warning them. The disaster has not yet arrived. The deathbed prophet for the nation of Israel is sounding the alarm. Will the mother turn from her whorings? Or will the Lord have to punish her?

Her Sins Identified (2:5)

God now identifies her sins. She *has played the whore*. She *acted shamefully*. She said, *"I will go after my lovers, who give me my bread and my water, my wool and my flax, my oil and my drink."* What does He mean by her lovers? Verse 13 tells us. She has *feast days of the Baals*—the false gods. These false gods are associated with the nations that she has looked to for her material prosperity. She's looked to those nations, and because she sees material prosperity as connected to their gods, she has also looked to their gods. Because of those idolatrous nations' prosperity, she has succumbed to all the sin and wickedness that is associated with that idolatry, including sacrifice of children and temple prostitution. Hosea's ministry follows what was a golden age of prosperity for the northern kingdom. The people have had plenty. They have also had peace. Assyria has been distracted by wars in other places. As a result, the raids into Israel have stopped, and Israel's borders have expanded in both the south and the north. However, the nation has seen its prosperity as coming not from the living God, but from the nations where they have had alliances, and from the gods associated with those nations. Ezekiel (chapter 16) spoke in a similar way to the southern kingdom of Judah concerning its alliances.

My own nation has been blessed materially, but we've said, "Our blessing hasn't come from the God of the Bible, the God we've heard about in the preaching of the gospel for many years. No, we are the explanation for our own prosperity. Capitalism and our treaties are the reasons for our prosperity." This is the same sort of thing that the northern kingdom of Israel was doing.

You may want to circle the word *my* every time it appears in verse 5. God will comment on that a few verses later. She thought her lovers (her idols) gave her everything—her food (*my bread, my water*, her clothing (*my wool, my flax*), her luxuries (*my oil, my wine*). She falsely attributes these things to the false gods of those nations whom she has run after. She has made trade alliances with surrounding nations, and she has seen her prosperity as the result of those alliances and the gods that were worshipped by those peoples.

GOD DETAILS THE JUDGMENTS (2:6-13)

God now walks Israel through the judgments that He has determined. He will divest her of what she has received from Him. This judgment is described in six ways.

Frustrated Desires (2:6-7)

The agreements that Israel has been able to make, and all the benefits that have come from those agreements, will end. She will be isolated, cut off from these lovers. She'll keep running after these things, but she will no longer be able to find them. God will put a *hedge* around her—not a hedge of protection, such as in the book of Job, but a hedge of *thorns* to block her way. Every step God is taking here has a loving motive. What He desires, and what He will accomplish, is the restoration of His marriage, and the first step of that is frustrated desire. She will eventually long to *return* to her *first husband.* This reminds us of the parable of the two sons (Luke 15:11-32).

Dried Up Resources (2:8-9)

She *did not know* that the Lord was the one *who gave her the grain, the wine, and the oil, and who lavished on her silver and gold.* Instead, *they used* these *for Baal.*

Exposure of Shame (2:10)

The Lord says He will *uncover her lewdness in the sight of her lovers.* No one will be able to stop Him from doing this. She will no longer be attractive to her lovers. A woman may run from her husband and seek after lovers. She may be attractive to them at first, but after they have used her up, she is nothing but someone to throw away. This is what God will do to His people: make her ugly in the sight of those whom she has pursued. They won't want her any longer.

Loss of Joy (2:11)

God will take away all the celebrations that have been taking place annually, monthly and weekly. He will *put an end to all her mirth.*

Destruction of Trusts (2:12)

God will take away the things she has most trusted in. Israel's *vines* and *fig trees* were famous. He would lay them waste. She said her *lovers* had given them to her, attributing her prosperity to something other than the Lord. The Assyrians will bring devastation and depopulation. The land that now has vines and fig trees and prosperity will become *a forest* wilderness overrun by *beasts* that *devour* whatever they find there.

Devastating Judgment (2:13)

The Lord will *punish her for the feast days of the Baals*, those days when she *burned offerings to them* and *adorned herself* and *went after her lovers* and *forgot* the Lord. This is willful forgetting. There are people who should know better, who have been taught better, and then willfully turn against what they know and adopt another position, refusing to acknowledge God and what he's already revealed.

PRINCIPLES FROM THIS PASSAGE

The Idolatrous Life Is Pictured

We have just seen a description of the idolatrous life. What does an idolatrous life look like?

- It's <u>running after false gods</u>, looking to something or someone other than the Lord as your chief love. It's looking elsewhere for your sense of satisfaction, for your pleasure, to supply what you don't believe God will supply.
- It's <u>not recognizing the true source of your blessings</u>. You may even say that your blessings come from Him, but it's idolatry if you don't live it.
- It's <u>spending God's blessings on that which dishonors Him</u>, taking your body, your work opportunities, and your relationships and wasting it all on things that pass away, instead of using it all for the service of Yahweh.
- It's <u>having no shame</u> for what is shameful in your life. In this passage, the kingdom is a shameless woman, not blushing as she puts on her jewels and chases after her lovers. Idolatry doesn't have the godly sorrow that leads to repentance (2 Cor. 7:10).
- It's <u>not recognizing individual responsibility in an idolatrous culture</u>. Idolatry doesn't see that our lives must be different from the lives of those around us.

- It's <u>claiming as your own what really belongs to God</u>. It doesn't see that everything belongs to Him and is to be used for Him.

Loving Judgment Is Displayed

- It often moves forward in stages. In this case, he spells out for Israel the stages that will occur.
- It desires repentance more than judgment. This is why God warns, *Plead with your mother. Plead…lest I strip her naked* (2:3).
- The stages are discernable. These steps do not always indicate judgment, but we tend to know when this is true in our own case.
    - ○ *Frustration of sinful desires.*
      You may get close to what you want; get just close enough to taste it, but God doesn't allow you to achieve it. Why not? Because it would lead you away from Him. God's chief ambition for you is not giving you what you desire. It's giving you what you need. It's giving you Himself.
    - ○ *Removal of what you have not appreciated and re-sponded to rightly.*
      When your blessings from God lead you away from Him, and you stubbornly persist in your own sinful way, He may begin to remove what you already have, giving only loss. He systematically and progressively takes away what you have put in His place, so that you might recognize Who was giving it to you. It was coming from God, not from your idols, not from yourself.
    - ○ *Devastation through destruction.*
      God allows you to feel the devastating effects of sin. Your lewdness is exposed. There's no hiding the fact that you've been judged.
    - ○ *Isolating you in order to secure you.*
      Your lovers no longer want you.

Why does God do all of this? Because love rebukes sin. Love doesn't agree with it and doesn't deal with it softly. Love makes sin uncomfortable, to save people from this devastation. Love is willing to wound in order to heal. Look at verse 7 again.

2:7 *She shall pursue her lovers but not overtake them,*
and she shall seek them but shall not find them.
Then she shall say, 'I will go and return to my first husband,
for it was better for me then than now.'

3
Wounding to Heal
(2:14-23)

Chapters 2 and 3 of Hosea move from judgment to hope. This second chapter has three *therefore* statements. The first two dealt with punishment: *Therefore I will hedge up her way with thorns* (2:6) and *Therefore I will take back my grain in its time* (2:9). We now come to the third *therefore* statement: *Therefore, behold, I will allure her...* It looks to a time beyond the first two, which pointed to judgment. This one points to the reason for the first two. <u>God is wounding Israel to heal her</u>. He will deal severely with His wayward wife, but it won't be permanent, and it isn't an ultimate rejection of her. This is loving discipline, done with a future relationship in mind. God is cutting Israel off, isolating her, so that one day He will take her back to Himself, and she will be faithful.

RENEWED FELLOWSHIP (2:14-15)

Here God's behavior toward Israel alludes to His care and their trust in Him at the time when He brought them out of Egypt.

Renewed Dependence (2:14)

Now there will be once again a sense of their dependence upon the Lord. It will be an intimate relationship, and there won't be any doubt Who her provider is.

Restored Blessing (2:15)

The word *Achor* means "trouble." This valley became significant early in Israel's history. There God made known the seriousness of sin and of holiness in His punishment of Achan, who had stolen a silver bar and a garment.[6]

Joshua 7:22 *So Joshua sent messengers, and they ran to the tent; and behold, it was hidden in his tent with the silver underneath. ²³ And they took them out of the tent and brought them to Joshua and to all the people of Israel. And they laid them down before the LORD. ²⁴ And Joshua and all Israel with him took Achan the son of Zerah, and the silver and the cloak and the bar of gold, and his sons and daughters and his oxen and donkeys and sheep and his tent and all that he had. And they brought them up to the Valley of Achor. ²⁵ And Joshua said, "Why did you bring trouble on us? The LORD brings trouble on you today." And all Israel stoned him with stones. They burned them with fire and stoned them with stones. ²⁶ And they raised over him a great heap of stones that remains to this day. Then the LORD turned from his burning anger. Therefore, to this day the name of that place is called the Valley of Achor.*

The place became known as the Valley of Achor, but now this place of devastating judgment will be the place of new beginnings, of hope. God's discipline will accomplish its purpose.

Revived Obedience (2:15)

This renewed fellowship also brings with it a renewal of obedience, as when the Lord first brought Israel out of Egypt. Jeremiah gives us another description of their first love:

Jeremiah 2:2 *"Go and proclaim in the hearing of Jerusalem, Thus says the LORD, 'I remember the devotion of your youth, your love as a bride, how you followed me in the wilderness, in a land not sown.'"*

---

[6] There's a nearly parallel incident early in the life of the church when Ananias and Sapphira lied about what they were giving to the Lord. Their lie was exposed, and they fell down dead. The Lord takes sin seriously. We are not loving when we don't take it seriously.

RENEWED FAITHFULNESS (2:16-20)

This passage speaks of renewed faithfulness. When will this be? Like many prophecies, this has multiple fulfillments. There's a partial fulfillment when Jews return from Babylon. There's further fulfillment when Christ comes and many are converted. Then there's the final, general conversion of Jews mentioned in Romans 9-11.

This faithfulness will not be explained by Israel, but by God. He will create a new, intimate relationship with them. Notice all the *I will* statements in this section.

- He will cure idolatries (2:16-17)
- He will create harmony (for Israel) (2:18a)
  During the millennial reign, this future day of faithfulness for Israel will be a day where all of creation reflects the harmony and peace that God produces in the lives of these people.
- He will cause them to dwell in safety. (2:18b)
- He will cause them to be a faithful people like they never have been before. (2:19-20)

This is also seen in Isaiah.

Isaiah 11:6-9 *The wolf shall dwell with the lamb,*
and the leopard shall lie down with the young goat,
and the calf and the lion and the fattened calf together;
and a little child shall lead them.
⁷ The cow and the bear shall graze;
their young shall lie down together;
and the lion shall eat straw like the ox.
⁸ The nursing child shall play over the hole of the cobra,
and the weaned child shall put his hand on the adder's den.
⁹ They shall not hurt or destroy
in all my holy mountain;
for the earth shall be full of the knowledge of the LORD
as the waters cover the sea.

This relationship is described in a beautiful way. It will be one of

- Love (*betroth*). A person is not betrothed midway into a marriage. God is saying that it won't be a patched-up relationship, but as if it's new.

31

- Exclusivity (*to Me*)
- Permanence (*forever*)
- Holiness (*righteousness*)
- *Justice*
- Covenant love (*steadfast love*, חֶסֶד (hesed))
- *Mercy*
- *Faithfulness*
- Knowledge of the Lord (*you shall know the* LORD)

He has made a promise regarding His people, and He will fulfill it.

A REVERSAL OF FORTUNES (2:21-23)

This is a beautiful, future picture of God sowing and establishing Israel once again. It's as if the whole creation is calling out, "How long until it is done?"

- The heavens will open upon the earth (2:21)
- The earth will grant the desire of the produce (2:22)
- The produce will answer the future of God's people (2:23)

Everything God has purposed to do for His wife, He will bring to pass, and all the crying out will be answered. The time period for the fulfillment of this prophecy is at the second coming of Christ. However, you could see earlier "pre-fillments," small tokens of the ultimate answer. It's true to say that with the Babylonian captivity, Israel was, in a sense, cured from her open idolatry. When she returned to the land, the days of open blatant Baal worship were virtually over.

Next, you could consider the first coming of our Lord. As a result of His life, death, and resurrection, there is the apostolic preaching of the gospel, and many Jews were converted at that time.

PRINCIPLES

The story of salvation is a story of grace.

The word *behold* in verse 14 calls us to see God's amazing love for His people. His love for us is no less amazing. Israel's unfaithfulness demonstrates the faithful love of God. God's love is explained solely by His determination to love them. Why would a man woo an unfaithful wife to himself? Why care for her after she has proven to be a traitor? Who wants a woman who runs after others instead of her husband? Humanly, it's not logical. But God's love does not follow man's logic. It flows from His grace.

In the mystery of providence, God uses judgment to bring salvation.

Consider the person who is running from God, ruining their life, stubborn, and unwilling to hear. As a result, God may allow them to feel the full force of their sinful ways. They are destroyed, divested of what He's given to them. They are stripped bare, with no way to hide their sin. Then God takes their *valley of trouble* and turns it into a *door of hope*, meeting them in their desperation. He does a powerful saving work of grace that no one expected. We can't fully understand it, but we see and experience it. Our marvelous God does such things.

Because of the grace of God and power of God, devastation can be the place where beauty is born.

I've met with many couples where there has been unfaithfulness in the marriage relationship. It's ugly. And yet, in some cases, those two people humble themselves and individually turn to the Lord, and as a result, they turn to each other in His presence. God takes that broken situation and turns it into a faithful, loving, lasting marriage. It becomes a relationship that honors the Lord and displays Christ, where before there was nothing that looked like Jesus. If you have come to a place of devastation in your life, then humble yourself and turn to the Lord. He can turn your *valley of trouble* into a *door of hope*. Watch what God does, because He is gracious, loving, good and kind.

4
A Story of Love and Redemption
(3:1-5)

This chapter illustrates God's lavish, incomprehensible love for Israel, despite her continuing adulterous behavior toward Him. We are loved in the very same way, but can't really understand the magnitude of our sin, or how scandalous, offensive and criminal it is to Him. Even as believers, when our spiritual senses are at their highest and our hearts are at their warmest, we barely get a glimpse of these two realities, and when we do, our hearts begin to feel overwhelmed. God must strengthen us just to give us a glimpse of the glory of His love and kindness towards us, and even then, it is beyond us. That is why God's word says...

2 Corinthians 9:15 *Thanks be to God for his inexpressible gift!*

Commenting on the Greek word translated *inexpressible*, Friberg's Analytical Greek Lexicon says, "of what cannot be told because it is too wonderful for words." Another has "pertaining to that which cannot be fully related or communicated." Similarly, Ephesians 3:8 speaks of *the unsearchable riches of Christ.* Someone compared this to tracking an animal higher and higher up into the mountains until you can't track it anymore; it's untraceable. Trying to comprehend God's love is like that.

LOVE'S CHOICE (3:1)

God has a story to tell about His love, and He is going to tell it in a way that men can begin to grasp by picturing it through the example of Hosea's love for his wife, Gomer.

Hosea is commanded by God to go somewhere, and his going represents his love for her. Gomer has lived like a prostitute. She took all of her husband's gifts and benefits and spent them on others. She left her husband, cutting herself off from him. Gomer would not listen to Hosea, so he has to appeal to her children to plead with their mother. God gave her over to effects of her sin—just as he would do later with Israel, and just as He still does today. From frustrated desires, to the systematic loss of what she possessed, to the open exposure of her sin, and finally to the unmistakable marks of devastation, this woman has been reduced to throwaway status.

Now, fully acknowledging that she has been an adulterous wife, God commands Hosea to go to her again and love her.

There is a translation question here regarding the words *another man*. The word in question is the Hebrew word רֵעַ (rê·aʻ) meaning companion, neighbor, or friend. It can be used to speak of a covenant relationship. It is used throughout the Ten Commandments and is translated *neighbor*, as in *Do not covet your neighbor's wife* (Ex. 20:17). The New American Standard takes this to refer to Hosea, her companion. That is, she *is loved by* her *husband*, even though she is an adulteress. It seems to parallel the next statement. The Lord loves Israel, even though Israel has committed spiritual adultery by worshiping other gods and offering cakes of raisins to the Baals. Others see this as Gomer having given herself to a neighbor. Regardless, Hosea is being told to go to her again and to love her.

This illustration of Hosea's love for Gomer provides some principles about love. One of the great tragedies in American Christianity is that we don't really think biblically, but culturally and emotionally. We have lost our way when it comes to the subject of love. It is not uncommon, even when talking to someone who has been well-taught in the Word of God, to hear them speak about love in emotional terms. "Well, I just don't know if I love that person anymore. I don't know if they love me anymore." Such talk reveals that people are thinking of love as just feelings.

Love can be chosen.

Love can be commanded by God, so love can be chosen. Why would Hosea love her?

- Not because of her love for him.
- Not because of her faithfulness to him.

- Not because of moral virtues.
- Not because she would make him look good. (What kind of respectable wife would he have now?)

Love can be for a higher cause, not just for ourselves.

Love can be for submission to God. We can love someone because we've been commanded to love. Yes, Gomer has been unfaithful to the covenant that she entered into with Hosea. But that doesn't mean that Hosea needs to be unfaithful to his side of the covenant. Just because your partner has been unfaithful to the covenant from their side, doesn't mean that you should be unfaithful to the covenant from your side, any more than Israel's unfaithfulness to God's covenant from her side wipes out God's commitment to her in terms His unconditional covenant.

Love can be full of forgiveness and mercy.

Hosea is a real man with emotions like us. Imagine how he feels when his wife leaves him, and it becomes common knowledge that she is playing the harlot. Imagine what it is like when she will not communicate with him, so that his only way of communicating with her is through the children, *Plead with your mother.* Imagine how he feels when he learns that she is being sold this day. Yet when God tells him to *Go again* and to *love* her, he obeys. For Hosea to love Gomer, he must forgive her. He cannot have vengeance in his heart, but mercy. Emotions were never intended by God to control the believer. The believer has control over emotion. Our obedience to God isn't based on emotion, but neither is it apart from emotion. We must sometimes choose despite the way we feel, and as we make obedient choices, the Lord changes the way we feel. We see things differently when we see them from His point of view.

LOVE'S PURCHASE (3:2)

Apparently, Gomer has become a slave, just a piece of property. In that day, there are several ways that someone can become a slave. Some have been captured in war or born into a slave's family. Others have become slaves through indebtedness, which is probably the way that Gomer became a slave.

She is humiliated in her sin, almost certainly stripped when she is sold.[7] This fulfills God's warning to Israel.

Hosea 2:3 *lest I strip her naked*
and make her as in the day she was born.

Obediently, Hosea redeems her, buying her for *fifteen shekels of silver* plus some *barley*. The price for a common slave is 30 shekels, so the silver plus the barley probably equals that. In the eyes of the public, she isn't anything special; not worth a special price

LOVE'S DEVOTION (3:3-4)

As Hosea pays the price, Gomer may be wondering, "Why is he doing this? Is he going to exact some revenge? Will he kill me? Will he turn me over to the punishment for adultery? Is he buying me to make me do demeaning service to pay for what I've done?" No, Hosea is buying Gomer to devote her to himself. Though he buys her as a slave, he's not going to treat her as a slave. She is to be his wife, and his alone, to love her and to be faithful to her. He doesn't treat her like a slave, but as a wife. He has proven himself to be worthy of her love but has had to purchase her for himself. Then she will learn to love him, and their relationship will be established.

- He takes her away for himself.
- He commands her to cease from her life of adultery.
- He commits himself to be faithful to her. *So will I also be to you.* Or as the New American Standard says, *toward you.* In keeping with the next verses, it appears that he will not be with her intimately until the *many days* are over, but he will certainly be faithful.

LOVE'S FAITHFULNESS (3:5)

The prophetic significance of what Hosea experienced is now revealed. This is a picture of what God will do with Israel. She is headed for a time of isolation, taken away from all that led to her apostasy from God. The Lord was her King, but she chose earthly kings instead and trusted in them. So now she will dwell without king or prince. Instead of pure worship of the

---

[7] Boice, pp. 34-35, and see Boice, "Sex, Marriage and Divorce,"
http://www.oneplace.com/ministries/the-bible-study-hour/read/articles/sex-marriage-and-divorce-10450.html

Lord, she has given herself to false gods. Now she will be without them—without these sacrifices and these ephods and these household gods. However, her re-gathering and redemption are not to destroy her. Rather, Israel will be betrothed to God in righteousness and faithfulness. This will not happen because she is faithful, but because He is faithful. Israel has not practiced covenant faithfulness, but God will be faithful to His covenant that He made with them. The result is that:

- They will *return.*
- Their heart will be changed. They *will seek the Lord their God, and David their king* (a reference to the Messiah).
- They will be united in submission and reverence. *They shall come in fear to the LORD.*
- *In the latter days,* all of this will come about not because of their faithfulness, but because of the Lord's *goodness.*

APPLYING IT

God commands Hosea to go to do this so that we would grasp something of the unbelievable, amazing love of God.

- This illustrates His unchanging love for Israel. It is also described in Romans 9-11. Paul asked, *Has God rejected His people?* (Romans 11:1) The answer is clear: *By no means!* There will be a literal nation of Israel during the Millennial Kingdom, redeemed people who seek the Lord their God and come to Him with trembling, who united in submission to their King David who is the Lord Jesus Christ. Even though she has been unfaithful, and still exists mostly in apostasy and unbelief, that day is coming. God will bring about what He has planned for this people in accordance with all the promises that He's made. He will bring it all to pass not because men are faithful, but because God is faithful. That's our God's love.
- This tells a story about marriage, covenant love, covenant faithfulness, and loving because we choose to. We love even when there's a cost, love even when we're not loved and even if there was unfaithfulness. In Ephesians 5:25, Christian marriage is compared to the way Christ loved the church.

- This tells a story about our own salvation. Do you recognize who we are in the story? We're not the Savior. We're not Hosea. Who are we in the story? We're Gomer. We should have loved Him first. He's worthy of our love. He has been nothing but good and faithful and kind to His creatures. Who wouldn't love someone like Him? But sinful man doesn't. We wander throughout the earth like a brazen woman trying to find satisfaction with all our lovers, becoming frustrated in our desires and systematically reduced to the place we hit rock bottom. One day, in the grace of God, we recognize that we are just a slave to sin. The language of redemption is the language of a purchase price. It is the story of a substitution, a redemption.

1 Corinthians 7:23 *You were bought with a price; do not become slaves of men.*

Acts 20:28 *Pay careful attention to yourselves and to all the flock, in which the Holy Spirit has made you overseers, to care for the church of God, which he obtained with his own blood.*

1 Peter 1 :18 *knowing that you were ransomed from the futile ways inherited from your forefathers, not with perishable things such as silver or gold, 19 but with the precious blood of Christ, like that of a lamb without blemish or spot.*

All of this teaches us how we must love. Since we have been shown such love, grace, and mercy, we must not refuse to love and to forgive. God has always been faithful to us, despite our moments of unfaithfulness. We have been loved by God, and that love deserves complete, wholehearted devotion.

5
God's Controversy with His People, Part 1
(4:1-19)

Hosea 4 is a wake-up call in the form of a legal prosecution. God is bringing a formal charge against Israel. God has a case, and He is making it known.

The Lord is detailing the people's sins. As we prepare to study this chapter, it's helpful to think about how the wicked person relates to sin. In the early verses of Psalm 36, David paints a portrait of the wicked person. This Psalm is already a couple of hundred years old in Hosea's time, so the people should be aware of it.

Psalm 36:1 To the choirmaster. Of David, the servant of the LORD.
Transgression speaks to the wicked deep in his heart;
there is no fear of God before his eyes.
2 For he flatters himself in his own eyes
that his iniquity cannot be found out and hated.
3 The words of his mouth are trouble and deceit;
he has ceased to act wisely and do good.
4 He plots trouble while on his bed;
he sets himself in a way that is not good;
he does not reject evil.

- He is <u>driven by sin</u>—his sin *speaks* to him, not God.
- He is <u>receptive to sin</u>—he listens to it. *Deep in his heart*, it is sin that has his ear.
- He is <u>proudly irreverent</u>. (4:1b-2)

- He is <u>recognized by his words</u>—they are *trouble and deceit*.
- He is <u>recognized by his wayward behavior</u>—it's now unwise instead of good.
- He <u>chooses evil</u> and <u>sets himself against the good way</u>. He chooses evil when he does not reject evil.

The wicked go their own way; the righteous trust in God's ways. The wicked man imagines that he will never have to give an account for any of his choices, or he thinks the day of judgment is so far out into the future that he has no fear of it, or he may just want to be left alone, imagining that he has no controversy with God. Maybe he doubts that God exists, and thinks he'll live life his own way, and then be done with it.

Hosea 4 is a wake-up call in the form of a legal prosecution. We could think of verse 1 as saying, "Hear ye, hear ye. The court is in session," because God is bringing a formal charge. *Hear the word of the Lord, O children of Israel, for the Lord has a controversy with the inhabitants of the land.* God has a case, and He is prosecuting it.

God serves notice to Israel, and to us. <u>One day, all those who arrogantly sin against God discover that God has a controversy with them</u>. One day, and it isn't always the final Day of Judgment, those who think God doesn't see, and doesn't care, discover that the living God has noticed their sin, and He takes action. Though God is patient beyond measure, He will not be patient forever. Sooner or later the day of reckoning arrives. There's payday someday.

GOD TAKES NOTE OF SIN (4:1-2)

If the people are unaware of their sins against God, and the gravity of those sins, God certainly isn't. He makes it known to them, formally charging them with sin on two levels.

God takes note of what is missing

God begins with their sins of omission. Many think of sin only in terms of actively doing wrong, rebellion against God's commands. But sin is also the absence of what God commands; it is indifference to God's commands.

Faithfulness

The word faithfulness (אֱמֶת 'emet) speaks of truth and firmness. Whether it is a verbal commitment, a contract, a marital commitment, or any other kind of commitment, the faithful person is firm. The sinful, unfaithful person is someone you can never pin down. If there is no firmness in their commitments, that is sin, and God takes note of it.

The faithfulness envisioned is first and foremost faithfulness to God. Any loyalty, whether within family, friendships, or even in your marriage, that would set you opposite to God's revealed will, is a perversion of faithfulness. True faithfulness in human relationships is acting in a way consistent with faithfulness to God.

Hosea has been living out a picture of God's faithfulness to His people. God has chosen to compare marriage to the relationship He has with His people. He's done that both in this book and elsewhere in His Word. So, Hosea has been called by God to be faithful to Gomer even though she has been unfaithful to him. His faithfulness to Gomer is rooted in his faithfulness to God. This is where all human faithfulness begins. Faithfulness is found when we strive to walk according to the example that God Himself has set. As God is faithful to His people, so we should be faithful to each other.

The faithfulness envisioned is also a general character quality. It is being trustworthy—not only toward family or toward people we like, but in all our relationships. It doesn't pick and choose its faithfulness, because ultimately, it's not faithfulness toward people, but toward God. It should be possible to say of any of us that there is nothing people could do that would move me away from my commitments to them, because that's how God deals with me.

Steadfast Love

This is covenant love, covenant commitment (חֶסֶד ḥesed). Israel is missing the love of choice that proves faithful toward its object. They are missing God's kind of love, a divine love that doesn't move away even in the face of mistreatment. It's the love that remains faithful, sacrificing and persevering. It is amazing what people will throw away in their sin—the ease with which people will devalue relationships and discard them.

The Knowledge of God

All of this reveals that they don't know God. When people truly know God, faithfulness and steadfast love matter to them, and they have godly character. When these characteristics are absent, it means the knowledge of God is absent. Those who know God realize *that he rewards those who seek him* (Heb. 11:6). They acknowledge His commands and His claims on their lives. But the people around Hosea have love that's fickle. What does God want?

Hosea 6:4 *What shall I do with you, O Ephraim? What shall I do with you, O Judah? Your love is like a morning cloud, like the dew that goes early away.* ⁵ *Therefore I have hewn them by the prophets; I have slain them by the words of my mouth, and my judgment goes forth as the light.* ⁶ *For I desire steadfast love and not sacrifice, the knowledge of God rather than burnt offerings.*

God doesn't want our sacrifices. He wants our lives. Going to church means nothing if your heart is not given to God. God not only wants us to have the knowledge of Him. He commands it.

Hosea 13:4 *But I am the LORD your God from the land of Egypt; you know no God but me, and besides me there is no savior.*

The statement *you know no God but me* has a jussive verb that's really a gentle command.⁸ The knowledge of God means both an acknowledgement of the reality of God and a right response to Him—to His character and to what He's done for us.

Remember that Hosea is the deathbed prophet to the nation of Israel, the last one sent to the northern kingdom before Assyria comes. The judgment of God is hanging above their heads and about to fall. Israel acknowledges His reality—she claims that she knows God and wants to know Him:

Hosea 8:2 *To me they cry, "My God, we* [Israel] *know you."*

But God doesn't deal with claims. He deals with reality:

Hosea 5:3 *I know Ephraim, and Israel is not hidden from me; for now, O Ephraim, you have played the whore; Israel is defiled.* ⁴ *Their deeds do not permit them to return to their God. For the spirit of whoredom is within them, and they know not the LORD.*

Hosea 11:1 *When Israel was a child, I loved him, and out of Egypt I called my son.* ² *The more they were called, the more they went away; they kept sacrificing to the Baals*

---

⁸ In grammar, a jussive verb is for commanding or exhorting. A number of translations take this verse as a command.

and burning offerings to idols. ³ *Yet it was I who taught Ephraim to walk; I took them up by their arms, but they did not know that I healed them.*

The people's unfaithfulness and selfishness are first manifested toward God, and then in their relationships with one another.

Before leaving this list of what is absent in their lives, we can each ask, "What is present in my life for the Lord? Am I pursuing the Lord? Do I know Him? Do I understand and display faithfulness to God and faithfulness in commitments to people? Do I show steadfast love?" It's possible to slide away from those things.

God takes note of what is present

Sin is not just the absence of what God commands; it is the presence of what He hates. What's present in the land?

- *Swearing* (cursing)—breaking the second commandment.
- *Lying*—breaking the ninth commandment.
- *Murder*—breaking the sixth commandment.
- *Stealing*—breaking the eighth commandment.
- *Committing adultery*—breaking the seventh commandment.
- *Violence*—The Lord says *they break all bounds.* It's not that they haven't been told what's wrong. They have the ten commandments. It's that they don't care.
- *Bloodshed*—literally, *bloody deed touches bloody deed.* It's as if there is one continual stream of bloodshed.

GOD TAKES ACTION CONCERNING SIN (4:3-11)

God doesn't ignore the sin that He sees.

God punishes sin

God punishes the sin. He visits it with discipline. Verse 3 begins with the word *therefore.* He makes a direct connection between their sins against

God and the negative things about to be described. Israel should not imagine that these troubles are just happening on their own.

Depression

The entire scene is a dark one. The *land mourns*, and the inhabitants *languish*. It is difficult, dark. There is no godly joy, no godly hope. One mark of the judgment of God is that we are given over to our depravity. Look at what is in the land according to verse 2. Compare that with the description of God's judgment in Romans chapter 1.

Romans 1:28 *And since they did not see fit to acknowledge God, God gave them up to a debased mind to do what ought not to be done. ²⁹ They were filled with all manner of unrighteousness, evil, covetousness, malice. They are full of envy, murder, strife, deceit, maliciousness. They are gossips, ³⁰ slanderers, haters of God, insolent, haughty, boastful, inventors of evil, disobedient to parents, ³¹ foolish, faithless, heartless, ruthless. ³² Though they know God's decree that those who practice such things deserve to die, they not only do them but give approval to those who practice them.*

We may see a society that's in the depths of degradation and say, "That deserves the judgment of God." It does, but that degradation is a part of God's judgment, when He gives a people up to their depravity.

Deprivation

Things are taken away. The *beasts* and the *birds* and even the *fish* are taken away. God's judgment is felt in the environment. The bottom line is that they work more but produce less. Sometimes this happens progressively, as if the Lord is crying out, "Will you listen to Me?" God demonstrates that they never provided for themselves in the first place.

Remember that they have been told in the Law to be alert for any man or woman turning away from God. Individual response matters, because sin is like leaven, like yeast (Galatians 5:9). It spreads.

Deuteronomy 29:18 *"Beware lest there be among you a man or woman or clan or tribe whose heart is turning away today from the LORD our God to go and serve the gods of those nations. Beware lest there be among you a root bearing poisonous and bitter fruit, ¹⁹ one who, when he hears the words of this sworn covenant, blesses himself in his heart, saying, 'I shall be safe, though I walk in the stubbornness of my heart.' This will lead to the sweeping away of moist and dry alike. ²⁰ The LORD will not be willing to forgive him, but rather the anger of the LORD and his jealousy will smoke against that man, and the curses written in this book will settle upon him, and the LORD will blot out his* *name from under heaven. [21] And the LORD will single him out from all the tribes of Israel for calamity, in accordance with all the curses of the covenant written in this Book of the Law. [22] And the next generation, your children who rise up after you, and the foreigner who comes from a far land, will say, when they see the afflictions of that land and the sicknesses with which the LORD has made it sick— [23] the whole land burned out with brimstone and salt, nothing sown and nothing growing, where no plant can sprout, an overthrow like that of Sodom and Gomorrah, Admah, and Zeboiim, which the LORD overthrew in his anger and wrath— [24] all the nations will say, 'Why has the LORD done thus to this land? What caused the heat of this great anger?' [25] Then people will say, 'It is because they abandoned the covenant of the LORD, the God of their fathers, which he made with them when he brought them out of the land of Egypt, [26] and went and served other gods and worshiped them, gods whom they had not known and whom he had not allotted to them. [27] Therefore the anger of the LORD was kindled against this land, bringing upon it all the curses written in this book, [28] and the LORD uprooted them from their land in anger and fury and great wrath, and cast them into another land, as they are this day.'*

[29] *"The secret things belong to the LORD our God, but the things that are revealed belong to us and to our children forever, that we may do all the words of this law."*

The people have been warned, but they have not listened.

Destruction

This sums up all of what's gone before. This destruction is not just physical. It's spiritual and moral destruction, and the whole nation is responsible, beginning with the spiritual leaders, but extending to the rest of the population.

Before we look at this in detail, consider some general principles.

APPLYING IT

It is fruitless to look horizontally when there is a vertical problem. (4:4a)

Verse 4 is difficult to render, as the various translations demonstrate. But it appears that God is saying that when all these difficulties arise due to the people's sins, they will want to turn against each other and contend with each other, as if that's the issue. But the issue is not a horizontal one. It's a vertical problem. The problem is their relationship to God.

The condition of the nation is one of rebellion. (4:4b)

Again, the second part of verse 4 is difficult to render, and the translations reflect that.

New American Standard: *Yet let no one find fault, and let none offer reproof; For your people are like those who contend with the priest.*

If that translation is right, Hosea is comparing the entire nation to those who cast off spiritual authority. What does the Law tell them about this?

Deuteronomy 17:12 *The man who acts presumptuously by not obeying the priest who stands to minister there before the LORD your God, or the judge, that man shall die. So you shall purge the evil from Israel.*

They are contending with someone much greater than a priest. They are contending with God. When you pursue sin, you're contending with God, and one day He will contend with you.

God holds everyone accountable and begins with those entrusted with leadership. (4:4-6)

The more you have been given, the more will be required of you. The people are guilty, but God begins His reproof with those who should be teaching the people truth but are not. Those in leadership have a weighty responsibility. This is true in the church (Heb. 13:17), in the family (Josh. 24:15; Eph. 6:4) and in the nation (Prov. 31:4). When Adam and Eve sinned, the serpent approached Eve first, but after they sinned, the Lord called to Adam, and He went on to say, "because you listened to the voice of your wife." God held Eve accountable, too, but He began with Adam, where the greater responsibility had first been entrusted. Incidentally, wives cannot use submission as an excuse for disobedience to God, because any submission should first be submission to the Lord God.

The people get the leaders they deserve. (4:9)

Like people, like priest indicates that the spiritual leadership matches the spiritual condition of the people. God judges a people by removing faithful leadership and giving them leaders who match their spiritual desires. Again, this is judgment. It is a great grace when God gives a people faithful leaders.

Don't wait for a deathbed prophet. Turn whole-heartedly to the Lord God this day and believe Him.

6
God's Controversy with His People, Part 2
(4:4-19)

GOD'S CHARACTER FROM THE POINT OF GRACE

God is prosecuting His people. What is most sobering and what should be most frightening is that God is not just the prosecuting attorney. He is the judge. When God brings a charge, no one else wins the case.

We have looked at the charges in their general form (4:1-4). Now God makes it more specific. He begins with the priests and the prophets (4:4-11), and then deals with the nation as a whole (4:12-19).

THE CASE AGAINST THE LEADERS (4:4-11)

Verse 5 appears to be addressed to *the priest* (see 4:6) and says *the prophet also shall stumble with you by night.* He may be referring to the high priest only, but probably to the priests and prophets in general—the spiritual leadership.

A General Pronouncement of Judgment (4:5)

There's no safe place. Both the priest and the prophets will stumble. There will be stumbling by day and by night. They will stumble—that is, they will come short of the goal of final blessing in the presence of God. They won't finish the race well, if at all. A New Testament contrast is in Jude.

Jude 24 *Now to him who is able to keep you from stumbling and to present you blameless before the presence of his glory with great joy ... .*

Jude pictures you standing before the Lord one day *with great joy*, and God has preserved His people. You have not stumbled. You've not been destroyed. But for these priests and prophets who have misled God's people, there's no such promise. The *priest* will be destroyed, as will his *mother*. By *mother*, he means the northern kingdom as a whole. Why will God destroy the mother? Why will they stumble?

Specific Sins and Specific Judgments

Now, God gets more specific in His charges against them.

Rejected responsibility means rejected opportunity (4:6a)

My people are destroyed for lack of knowledge. We saw that earlier. There's a lack of the knowledge of God in the land. They don't know the Lord. Although they will bear individual responsibility for that, the leaders also have a responsibility for their not knowing the Lord. He's addressing the priests and the prophet when he says, *because you have rejected knowledge, I reject you from being a priest to me.*

Some people believe that in 4:6, the Lord is switching from addressing the priests to addressing the northern kingdom as a whole. They see this verse as saying that Israel will no longer serve as a priest to the nations: Israel rejected the knowledge of the Lord, so the Lord will destroy them, and they will no longer serve as a priest to the nations. That's no doubt true, but it seems better to see this entire section as continuing the same topic: God is addressing the leadership here. They have failed to teach the people the truth, and therefore, they will be removed. They will no longer have the privilege and the responsibility.

Willful forgetfulness means being forgotten (4:6b)

The judgments match the sins. Because they have *forgotten* the law of their God, He will forget their children. The people's future will be bleak; a future of destruction because they have walked away from God's law. For God to remember them is for God to protect them and supply for them. For God to *forget* them is to leave them to what their sins deserve.

Wasted influence means loss of influence (4:7)

The more they (these priests) *increased, the more they sinned against me; I will change their glory into shame.*

What does it mean that *they increased?* It may mean that they increased in number. As priests were multiplied, all that happened as a result was that sin was multiplied. In the life of the northern kingdom, in the midst of all of this immorality and spiritual adultery, priests truly were multiplied. Jeroboam was king in the north, and he didn't want his people going up to Jerusalem in the southern kingdom to worship.

1 Kings 12:26 *And Jeroboam said in his heart, "Now the kingdom will turn back to the house of David.* ²⁷ *If this people go up to offer sacrifices in the temple of the* LORD *at Jerusalem, then the heart of this people will turn again to their lord, to Rehoboam king of Judah, and they will kill me and return to Rehoboam king of Judah."* ²⁸ *So the king took counsel and made two calves of gold. And he said to the people, "You have gone up to Jerusalem long enough. Behold your gods, O Israel, who brought you up out of the land of Egypt."* ²⁹ *And he set one in Bethel, and the other he put in Dan.* ³⁰ *Then this thing became a sin, for the people went as far as Dan to be before one.* ³¹ *He also made temples on high places and appointed priests from among all the people, who were not of the Levites.*

Jeroboam made two calves of gold. He set one up in Bethel and the other in Dan, both in the northern kingdom. He told the people that the calves were their gods who brought them up out of the land of Egypt, and the people sinned by worshiping them. He made temples on the high places and appointed priests, ordinary people who were not Levites. Just anybody could be a priest. As the number of illegitimate priests *increased*, the idolatrous worship increased.

They increased could also mean that they increased in honor, influence, and material gain. There was increased influence, but the influence hasn't been used for holy purposes. Rather, it's been used for increased sinning. They have glory now, but the Lord *will change their glory into shame.*

Rejoicing in sin means misery in sin (4:8-11)

If you rejoice in sin, taking pleasure in it, you will become miserable in it. Instead of confronting the people with God's truth and calling for repentance, the priests and the prophets *feed on the sin* of the Lord's people. They are *greedy for their iniquity.* The more the people sin, the better these priests think it is, because the priests are driven by self-interest. It's not too different today. In many cases, the most popular preachers, the wealthiest preachers, are those who refuse to address the sins of people. People desire sin, and the prophets tell them what they want to hear, benefitting from it. In fact, in many cases, they are greedy for the people to be greedy because they play on their greed to enrich themselves. "You want to be wealthy? Give to me. You want to be healthy? Give to the ministry. Sow your seed, and God will return a thousand-fold blessing."

They will be miserable because of it. 4:9 *And it shall be like people, like priest*... The Lord will *punish* and *repay* them for what they have done. Their spiritual adultery won't help. One of the things associated with Baal worship is fertility. The idea is that as you engage in these sacrifices, and as you engage in this cultic prostitution, it leads to fertility for the land. Hosea says in 4:10, *They shall eat, but not be satisfied; they shall play the whore but not multiply*....

These people *have forsaken the LORD to cherish whoredom, wine and new wine*. They cherish a life of wanton pleasure. For Who should be cherished, counted as precious? Do we understand that to love the Lord our God is to cherish Him, to understand His worth? Whatever is most important to us is what is most valuable to us. If God is not our priority, it's because we don't value Him as we should.

THE CASE AGAINST THE NATION (4:12-19)

The problem is broader than the leaders. The punishment will be *like people, like priest* (4:9). In fact, people tend to get the leaders they deserve. Leadership often reflects the spiritual condition of the people because they're not willing to hear the leaders they need. And therefore, just as we see in the New Testament, with itching ears we gather to ourselves the leaders who will tell us something that will allow us to live the way we want to live. The Lord sees sickness from the head to the toe, from the leaders all the way down.

By Addressing Israel Directly (4:12-14)

At the end of 4:11, He mentioned *wine* and *new wine* that *take away understanding*. Now, when He turns His attention to the people as a whole in verse 12, He begins with that lack of understanding. What are Israel's sins?

Sorcery (4:12)

Note the foolishness of false worship

Here's a complete lack of understanding: looking to *a piece of wood* for your answers. We don't know exactly how *their walking staff gives them oracles*. Some say you would drop it, and the various ways it might fall would give you answers that you were looking for. But regardless of the specifics, it is foolish superstition in the place of seeking the Lord.

Note the spiritual nature of false worship

Why do people turn from the true and living God to look for their guidance in this realm where an idol cannot see, cannot hear, and cannot speak? God says *a spirit of whoredom has led them astray.* That is very close to saying that they are demonically inspired. Remember that the New Testament tells us that things offered to idols are offered to demons (1 Cor 10:20). What we can say with absolute confidence is that it's a heart issue, whether a demonic spirit of whoredom or a mindset of whoredom. God says it has to do with their spirit. When a person goes astray with their feet, it cannot be explained by natural things. It must be explained by spiritual things. It's because they have gone astray in their heart. All false teaching has its source: Satan and his demons.

They have left their God to play the whore. The word *whore* is used over and over in this passage. We'd like God to soften it, but He doesn't. When we walk away from the Lord, that is how ugly, how distasteful it is. It's being a spiritual adulterer or adulteress.

Sacrifices to false gods (4:13a)

The false worship of Baal involves high places and groves and trees. The one thing all these trees have in common is shade. It's not clear whether the Lord's reference to the *shade* being *good* is sarcastic, or whether they see this shade as being part of their worship in some way.

Sexual immorality in the way of false worship (4:13b-14)

The word *therefore* tells us that there is a connection between their false worship and what happens with the next generation. The parents have gone astray from Yahweh. It's no wonder, then, that their children have gone astray—that their *daughters play the whore* and their *brides ... commit adultery.* Parents, don't assume that you can influence your children to walk a godly course that you won't walk. God may be merciful. Your children may love the Lord though you haven't. But it's often like father, like son. People figuratively sacrifice to their false gods and wonder why their children don't have a heart for the true God.

What is the meaning of the lack of punishment in verse 14? He may be telling the men that they are as responsible as the women are. They must not imagine that God will judge only the daughters and brides, and leave the men unpunished, when they are engaging in the very same sin. The men will be punished along with them; *a people without understanding shall come to ruin.*

Or, this may be saying that God can simply let the sin do its own punishing. A preacher years ago said that we don't realize that sin is its own best avenger. God has set laws into effect. When you take fire into your bosom, your clothes will be burned (Prov. 6:27). If you sow to the flesh, you will reap corruption (Gal. 6:8). Bad company corrupts good morals (1 Cor. 15:33). These are the sorts of things that God has said are in place, and He ensures that they stay in place.

By Addressing Israel Indirectly, Warning Judah about Israel (4:15-19)

God shames Israel by telling Judah to avoid her. He's basically saying that Israel's gone. In fact, as verse 17 says, *Ephraim* [the northern kingdom] *is joined to idols. Leave him alone.* One way that God calls to repentance is to command and exhort the one in sin to turn from sin. But another way that God calls to repentance is to warn the ones not in sin to avoid those who are sinning. In other words, God uses separation to call for consecration.

He warns them not to enter *Gilgal* nor to go up to *Beth-aven.* These were the religious centers in the northern kingdom. Beth-aven is a substitute for Beth-el. Beth-el means House of God. Beth-aven means House of Deceit or House of Lies. It's the place where Jacob had the vision of the ladder extended into heaven. He named it Bethel, the House of God, and swore an oath to the Lord there (Gen 28:10-22). But now God is saying not to go there, because these holy places have been transformed into unholy places through the false worship of these false gods. He warns them not to go there to swear an oath to Him.

In 4:16, God compares Israel to a stubborn heifer. A *heifer* is a cow (female) that has not yet borne a calf. God can do anything He wants, but He will never act in a way that's contrary to His own nature. He won't treat a stubborn heifer like a lamb. If you turn a stubborn ear to God, don't expect His blessings. He won't feed you *like a lamb in a broad pasture.* In fact, if you are one of His children, what you can expect is discipline.

Verse 17 is frightening. *Ephraim* (the northern kingdom) has become *joined to idols. Leave him alone.* There comes a time when God will pull back godly influence from a person or from a nation. That's a part of His judgment, and all that's left is judgment.

The northern kingdom is so corrupted that *when their drink is gone, they give themselves to whoring* (4:18). Even in the physical realm, people often live sexually immoral lives tied to alcohol. They drink, get drunk, and then give themselves to things that they may not have given themselves to otherwise.

But this people is so far gone that even after their drink is all gone, they still go to whoring. They no longer need the drink to help them do it. They know what they're doing. In fact, *their rulers dearly love shame*, because they profit from it.

But even when people live in sin and know they're living in sin, they are deceived. *A wind has wrapped them in its wings* (4:19). That is, they have been enveloped by a force, wrapped up and taken captive by sin.[9] That's what has happened when you know, see, hear, and are warned that your sin will destroy you, but you will not leave it. You find that what you have willingly given yourself to, thinking you are acting in freedom, has now turned you into a slave.

The end of it all will be shame. If you pursue sin and think you're getting away with it, you'll have to answer for it one day, and what is shameful will be clearly shown to be shameful.

APPLYING IT

- Concerning the <u>virtues</u> Israel lacks in Hosea's day
  - Are we faithful?
  - Do we have covenant love, God's kind of love that cannot be severed?
  - Do we have the knowledge of God, which is indicated by having faithfulness and covenant love?
- Concerning the <u>attitudes</u> that characterize Israel in her vices
  - Are we rebellious?
  - Are we stubborn, unwilling to listen to the Lord, unwilling to be guided by Him?
  - Do we take pleasure in sin?
  - Are we unfaithful to God, playing the whore spiritually?
- Concerning our <u>use of entrusted responsibility and increased influence</u>
  - Are we being faithful to teach His Word in our families?

---

[9] A second possible interpretation is that they have been wrapped up in deception, in things that are no more substantial than the wind. A third is that, though the Lord bore them on eagles' wings and brought them to Himself when He delivered them from Egypt, now it's as if they're carried in a whirlwind to destruction and shame.

○ Are we leading our families?

○ Are we walking according to the Word of God, being living examples of what it means to be God-lovers?

○ As God gives us open doors and the ability to influence others, are we using that for the sake of His name? Do we see that we should be faithful with these open doors?

Hebrews 12:1 *Therefore, since we are surrounded by so great a cloud of witnesses, let us also lay aside every weight, and sin which clings so closely, and let us run with endurance the race that is set before us, 2 looking to Jesus, the founder and perfecter of our faith*
....

Will we lay aside our sin, remembering that Jesus compared it to a willful dismemberment? *If your eye causes you to sin, pluck it out. If your hand offends you, cut it off.* It's better to go into the Kingdom maimed, than to go with a full body into hell. We so want to hold onto our sins, but they are dragging us to hell. What shall it profit a man if he gains the whole world and forfeits his soul? Or what will a man give in exchange for his soul?

Let us turn from our sins in all their forms before God's judgment falls.

7
God's Character and Judgment
(5:1-15)

GOD'S CHARACTER FROM THE POINT OF GRACE

The character of God is beautiful to those who have met Him on the ground of grace. His attributes are our comfort and our peace. Consider, for example:

- **God's commitment to justice.** He has accomplished our full and free forgiveness. He could not forgive us by turning a blind eye to justice. Instead, He accomplished full justice by punishing His Son for our sins to His complete satisfaction. God is both just and the justifier of the ungodly. This forgiveness is a reason to celebrate.
- **God's omnipotence** is our comfort and peace because it is by His power that we have been delivered from the domain of darkness and are kept safe.

Romans 8:31 *What then shall we say to these things? If God is for us, who can be against us?*

- **God's omniscience** is our comfort and peace because He knows those who are His, and He knows how to keep us safe. We also rest in the knowledge that He knows our true spiritual condition.

John 21:17 … *Peter was grieved because he said to Him the third time, "Do you love me?" and he said to Him, "Lord you know everything; you know that I love you."*

2 Peter 2: *7 and if he rescued righteous Lot, greatly distressed by the sensual conduct of the wicked.*

2 Peter 2: *9 then the Lord knows how to rescue the godly from trials, and to keep the unrighteous under punishment until the day of judgment …*

- **God's hatred of sin and commitment to righteousness** is our hope. We look forward to a world in which righteousness will dwell, with the King of Righteousness reigning on the earth.

2 Peter 3:13 *But according to his promise we are waiting for new heavens and a new earth in which righteousness dwells.*

GOD'S CHARACTER FROM THE POINT OF JUDGMENT

The fifth chapter of Hosea presents God's attributes as He exercises them in judgment. He sounds a warning to those who have not met with Him on the terms of peace and don't know Him through faith in His Son, the Lord Jesus Christ. He's the same God always, and the same attributes that are beautiful and encouraging to those who stand in grace, are dreadful to those who don't stand in grace. They are all reasons to be afraid. To be clear, there is no hope for those who don't repent.

Just because you say that you will meet Him on the ground of grace, doesn't mean that you will. In Hosea's day, righteousness and justice are glaringly lacking in the land of Israel. No matter what they are saying, and no matter the public demonstration of worship, the truth is being told by their heart condition and by their behavior. Amos, living at the same time as Hosea, describes those who say that they desire the Day of the Lord, but they don't know what they are asking for. There are many people who would say, "I'm looking forward to the Day of the Lord," who are in no position to be looking forward to it. They just don't realize it. One day it will be revealed that Jesus doesn't know them. That is already being revealed by their lives, by their thoughts and words, and by their lack of interest in the things of God. All these things are telling the truth, if they would just pay attention.

Amos 5:18 *Woe to you who desire the day of the LORD! Why would you have the day of the LORD? It is darkness, and not light, 19 as if a man fled from a lion, and a bear met him, or went into the house and leaned his hand against the wall, and a serpent bit him. 20 Is not the day of the LORD darkness, and not light, and gloom with no brightness in it? 21 "I hate, I despise your feasts, and I take no delight in your solemn assem-*

blies. 22 Even though you offer me your burnt offerings and grain offerings, I will not accept them; and the peace offerings of your fattened animals, I will not look upon them. 23 Take away from me the noise of your songs; to the melody of your harps I will not listen. 24 But let justice roll down like waters, and righteousness like an ever-flowing stream."

GOD'S BLIND COMMITMENT TO JUSTICE (5:1-2)

By a "blind commitment to justice," we mean that He is no respecter of persons. It makes no difference who you are, what your race is, nor your status in this world. If your deeds call for judgment, the Lord judges. The whole nation will be judged, but He singles out two groups: the *priests*, leaders in the religious realm and the *king*, leader in the political realm. Whether you're talking about the nation's leadership in religion, its political leadership, or the common man, God shows no partiality. When God was here on earth, this was one of the recognizable characteristics of His personality, something that even His enemies noticed.

Matthew 22:15 *Then the Pharisees went and plotted how to entangle him in his words. 16 And they sent their disciples to him, along with the Herodians, saying, "Teacher, we know that you are true and teach the way of God truthfully, and you do not care about anyone's opinion, for you are not swayed by appearances. 17 Tell us, then, what you think. Is it lawful to pay taxes to Caesar, or not?"*

Both **Mizpah** and **Tabor** are places where the false worship of the Baals has probably been happening. Instead of rescuing the people from false worship, the leaders have allowed these places to turn into *a ne*t for the feet of their people, *a snare* for the nation.

And the revolters have gone deep into slaughter—The true nature of false worship is rebellion against God. A couple of pictures may be communicated here. One is the idea that their sacrifices to the false gods, the Baals, have been multiplied, a picture of slaughter. Or, it may be that these leaders, by not rescuing people from false teaching, have actually slaughtered the people.

GOD'S PERFECT AND COMPLETE KNOWLEDGE (5:3-5)

He perfectly and completely knows the sin and disobedience of those who deserve to be judged by Him, knowing not only what they have done, but exactly what motivates their deeds and attitudes. Men may lie about their motives, they may even deceive themselves about their motivations, but God will not be informed by THEM. He will always be informed by Himself. God is omniscient—whatever you think is hidden in your life, you need to recognize that it's not hidden from God. When the Lord looks at them, what does He see?

- A *snare*, a *net spread*
- A nation in revolt
- Spiritual defilement
- Unwillingness to abandon their sins, so they are not able to *return* to God
- Ignorance of the true God—Hosea 4:1b: *There is no truth or knowledge of God in the land.*
- Pride before God's face

GOD'S IMMANENCE AND TRANSCENDENCE (5:6)

The Immanence of God

God can be sought and can be found. He is **everywhere.** This is different from pantheism, which says that God is **everything.** God has chosen to make Himself known to His creatures. He can be known, and His accepting presence can be experienced.

Jeremiah 29:13 *You will seek me and find me, when you seek me with all your heart.*

Amos 5:6 *Seek the LORD and live, lest he break out like fire in the house of Joseph, and it devour, with none to quench it for Bethel...*

The Transcendence of God

But God is not a part of what He has created, nor is He captured within the boundaries of His creation. Just as God can make Himself known, or not, He can choose to allow men to have an experience of Himself, or He can choose to withhold that same experience.

Isaiah 55:6 *"Seek the LORD while he may be found; call upon him while he is near;* [7] *let the wicked forsake his way, and the unrighteous man his thoughts; let him return to the LORD, that he may have compassion on him, and to our God, for he will abundantly pardon.* [8] *For my thoughts are not your thoughts, neither are your ways my ways, declares the LORD.* [9] *For as the heavens are higher than the earth, so are my ways higher than your ways and my thoughts than your thoughts.*

The idea here in Hosea 5:6 seems to be that even though you bring flocks and herds to make sacrifice and seek the Lord's face, you won't find Him. You don't find God when you're ready. You find God on the ground of His grace when God makes Himself known to you, and you simply respond to His initiative.

Being ready to respond is a true work of the Spirit of God. You respond because God has done a work in your heart. It is a mercy to know Him in forgiveness, to know Him as Father, Savior, Lord, and King. Seek the Lord while He may be found, because that offer of mercy may not be there in the same way tomorrow.

EXPRESSIONS OF GOD'S IRRESISTIBLE POWER (5:7-15)

God's Power Is Felt in Impending Destruction (5:7-9)

Instead of celebration and worship to God, the festivals should be gatherings for warnings because the judgment of God is imminent. He calls for more judgment because they're an idolatrous people. God will not bless them but will devour their fields.

Blow the horn in Gibeah, etc., is a call for battle. This is divine sarcasm, picturing the Benjamites leading out in battle. God is telling them to sound the alarm because it is coming like a train bearing down on them in the form of the Assyrian armies. This warning of destruction is a certainty.

God's Power Is Felt Like a Flood (5:10-11)

The leaders of the southern kingdom have become like land thieves who move boundaries. It may mean that they are thinking of the destruction of the northern kingdom and are hoping to move into that territory. Maybe they are stealing land from the common people. Or maybe it is saying that they are giving to idols what belongs to the Lord.[10] At any rate, they are doing what is accursed.

Deuteronomy 27:17 *"'Cursed be anyone who moves his neighbor's landmark.' And all the people shall say, 'Amen.'*

---

[10] See Albert Barnes, *Notes on the Bible* (various publishers and editions).

Ephraim traded purity for filth. Therefore, God's flood of power means their oppression and being crushed in judgment.

Psalm 32:6 *Therefore, let everyone who is godly offer prayer to you in a time when you may be found; Surely in the rush of great waters they shall not reach him.*

Psalm 93:1 *The LORD reigns; he is robed in majesty; the LORD is robed; he has put on strength as his belt. Yes, the world is established; it shall never be moved. ² Your throne is established from of old; you are from everlasting. ³ The floods have lifted up, O LORD, the floods have lifted up their voice; the floods lift up their roaring. ⁴ Mightier than the thunders of many waters, mightier than the waves of the sea, the LORD on high is mighty!*

God's Power Is Felt in Deprivation (5:12)

God judges not only by overwhelming, but He judges by taking away blessings, sometimes slowly. They lose everything they've traded for.

Psalm 39:11 *When you discipline a man with rebukes for sin, you consume like a moth what is dear to him; surely all mankind is a mere breath! Selah*

Isaiah 51:7 *"Listen to me, you who know righteousness, the people in whose heart is my law; fear not the reproach of man, nor be dismayed at their revilings. ⁸ For the moth will eat them up like a garment, and the worm will eat them like wool; but my righteousness will be forever, and my salvation to all generations."*

There is a choice: follow the Lord or be accepted by men.

God's Power Is Felt Like an Incurable Disease (5:13)

The northern kingdom went to the king of Assyria and tried to make a pact with him. Instead of looking to God, they looked to men, an effort to cure their wound in their own way. They didn't recognize that their real problem was not a political or a military one, but one of sin.

God's Power Is Felt Like a Devouring Lion (5:14-15)

God's power is like being given up to a lion. There will be nobody to help you.

Psalm 2:1 *Why do the nations rage and the peoples plot in vain? ² The kings of the earth set themselves, and the rulers take counsel together, against the LORD and against* *his Anointed, saying,* ³ *"Let us burst their bonds apart and cast away their cords from us."* ⁴ *He who sits in the heavens laughs; the Lord holds them in derision.* ⁵ *Then he will speak to them in his wrath, and terrify them in his fury, saying,* ⁶ *"As for me, I have set my King on Zion, my holy hill."* ⁷ *I will tell of the decree: The* LORD *said to me, "You are my Son; today I have begotten you.* ⁸ *Ask of me, and I will make the nations your heritage, and the ends of the earth your possession.* ⁹ *You shall break them with a rod of iron and dash them in pieces like a potter's vessel."*

GOD'S OFFER OF HOPE (5:15)

There is hope if you do not want to meet God in judgment. At the end of Chapter 5 we read, *I will return ...* ***UNTIL*** *they acknowledge their guilt and seek my face and in their distress earnestly seek me."*

The Attitudes

1. Honesty—the need to be truthful about your sin.
2. Earnestness—a genuine desire to be freed from sin.

The Actions

1. Acknowledge your guilt
2. Seek God's mercy and forgiveness

Why do we seek Him? What do we hope to find? We'll see that in the next chapter.

8
Repentance that Brings Hope
(6:1-3)

In previous chapters we've seen God's judgments upon His people because they are a spiritually adulterous people, but He still has a plan for ethnic Israel. God has made unconditional promises regarding the descendants of Abraham, and He will bring them to pass.

God's judgment has a purpose, which is Israel's ultimate repentance and salvation. This is why, in chapter 6:1-3, there is a sudden shift from judgment to hope. It is as if we are fast-forwarded, catapulted into the future, hearing the voice of Israel in the day when salvation has arrived.

6:1-3 pictures the nation when it has repented, and Israel recognizes who God really is. She has met with God's true character in judgment, and now she will rely on God's true character for her hope.

There is some debate about the true nature of this repentance. Some commentaries say that since there is no specific mention of their sins in verses 1-3, they almost expect the kindness of God automatically: like each new dawn, the coming of the spring rains and the later rains. God has met with them in judgment, so He will meet with them in mercy. Therefore, there's no real repentance.

However, I believe verses 1-3 give a clear picture of genuine repentance and a future hope for the nation. These verses are a continuation of thought from chapter 5, verse 15, when the people of Israel acknowledge their guilt, seek His face, and in their distress will earnestly seek Him. This is the rest of the picture and is what true repentance looks like.

REPENTANCE RECOGNIZES ESTRANGEMENT (6:1)

Notice how these verses begin: *Come, let us return to the LORD....* Hosea is not speaking. This is either the priests addressing the people, or the people talking among themselves. There is the recognition that a return is needed, that we are not on the right terms with God. If this repentance represents initial salvation, then there is the recognition of our lost condition, and we never have had true fellowship with God. If the repentance is on the part of a believing people, then there is the recognition that we have walked in a way contrary to His will. In other words, there can be no repentance until we recognize our waywardness. There can be no repentance when we are:

- Diminishing our sin
- Excusing our sin
- Blaming others for our sin
- Looking at anyone or anything else but our own sin

When this day of repentance comes, Israel will recognize what her sin has been—the rejection of her Messiah.

Zechariah 12:10 *"And I will pour out on the house of David and the inhabitants of Jerusalem a spirit of grace and pleas for mercy, so that, when they look on me, on him whom they have pierced, they shall mourn for him, as one mourns for an only child, and weep bitterly over him, as one weeps over a firstborn."*

Your only hope is salvation through faith in God's Son, but that is not possible unless you realize that this is what you need, and you acknowledge it.

REPENTANCE RECOGNIZES HIS JUDGMENT

Verse 1 is a continuation of the thoughts from chapter 5:14-15. God said, *I, even I, will tear them and go away.* Here, Israel says *Come and let us return to the LORD, for He has torn us, that he may heal us.* It further says, *He has struck us down.*

It is amazing how men can imagine that there is a disconnect between how poorly they are doing and their sins against God. Men are not only blind to their sins, but often blind to the divine judgments against their sins. God judges a person's sin in many ways. He judges

- in their thinking – fear, dread, dissatisfaction
- in their bodies – sickness, weakness
- upon their efforts – no blessing
- upon their environment – things are not favorable: weather, politics, war
- in their relationships – things fall apart

Notice that Israel will not see her wars, her defeats, the devastation of her land, and all the rest as random acts, but divine acts. These things don't just happen; it is God's judgment.

A word of caution—We should not say that every difficulty in one or more of these areas is judgment for sin. Job met with many of these things, and it was simply a proving ground.

REPENTANCE RECOGNIZES THAT HIS JUDGMENT IS JUST (6:1)

Israel recognizes His judgment, yet there is no blame in what they say. This recognition doesn't drive them away from God or make them resentful, but drives them to Him. That must mean that they can see that God's judgment was just: *Let us return to Him.* Notice David's confession in the NET Bible:

Psalm 51:4 *Against you – you above all – I have sinned; I have done what is evil in your sight. So you are just when you confront me; you are right when you condemn me.*

REPENTANCE RECOGNIZES GOD'S LOVINGKINDNESS (6:1-2)

Even more than the recognition that His judgment is just, there is the recognition that it has a loving end. This is not presumptive, but a realization of God's gracious character, *He has struck us down, and will bind us up.* The only One Who can be our Physician is the One Who has wounded us. The only One Who can heal us is the One who has torn us. Not only is He the only One who can do it; He is also willing to do it. He does not owe us a loving end, nor do we deserve God's love. Only a truly repentant heart would ever recognize this.

Not an Excuse for Sin

The heart is so deceptive that it will attempt to leave the impression that it is flattering God by not repenting. Men will even try to use God's holiness as an excuse to remain in their sins. For example, a deceptive heart says:

- God is too holy to receive someone like me.
- My sin has gone too far for there to be any forgiveness.
- God may forgive others, but others haven't done what I have done.

In truth, when people say these things, they haven't known repentance at all. True repentance sees not only the greatness of our sin, but it stands amazed at the greatness of God's grace. To know God, is to be confident that there is nothing too great for His forgiveness if we turn to Him with a true and broken heart.

REPENTANCE RECEIVES GOD'S GRACIOUS PROMISES (6:2-3)

God's gracious promises are as certain as His promises of judgment. The only way you ever meet with God in judgment is because of the stubborn sinfulness of your own heart. He tells you He will forgive and receive, and pleads with you to repent and live, swearing by His own character and nature.

Israel's confidence is based upon God's **declared** purposes. It is not a presumptuous confidence, nor does it presume that forgiveness is offered indiscriminately. Or, to put it another way, where the Holy Spirit grants a repentant heart, there is neither presumption, nor is there an underestimation of God's grace. There is a confidence based upon the Lord's statements. Just as God's judgment on the unrepentant is certain, where there's true repentance, His forgiveness is certain. He will restore.

God's declared purpose concerning Israel.

They believe that He forgives and that there is a future for their nation. That is why they say:

> *Let us know; let us press on to know the LORD; his going out is sure as the dawn; he will come to us as the showers, as the spring rains that water the earth.*

This is predictable. They have certainty: If we earnestly press on to know the Lord, he will *heal.* He will *bind us up.* It's as sure as the rising of the sun tomorrow, or as this text says, as certain as the coming of the spring rains.

God's declared passion for saving sinners.

He is interested not only in the well-being of Israel, but of all people. We can see this in several places in the book of Ezekiel.

Ezekiel 18:23 *Have I any pleasure in the death of the wicked, declares the Lord GOD, and not rather that he should turn from his way and live?*

Ezekiel 18:32 *For I have no pleasure in the death of anyone, declares the Lord GOD; so turn, and live."*

Ezekiel 33:11 *Say to them, As I live, declares the Lord GOD, I have no pleasure in the death of the wicked, but that the wicked turn from his way and live; turn back, turn back from your evil ways, for why will you die, O house of Israel?*

Hosea 6:1-3 is a picture of a future day of salvation, but it relates to a present day of salvation, because this is what repentance always looks like. There's the recognition that you're estranged from God. There's the recognition of God's judgment on sin…that things haven't been going well with you, and that it's not accidental; that it's connected to your rebellion against God. There's the recognition that His judgment on your sin is just. And there's knowledge of His lovingkindness and of the certainty of His promises of forgiveness and restoration for those who repent from sins and who turn to Him.

Through Hosea we have seen God's character in judgment and in hope. We see this also in the second Psalm.

Psalm 2:10 *Now therefore, O kings, be wise; be warned, O rulers of the earth.* [11] *Serve the Lord with fear, and rejoice with trembling.* [12] *Kiss the Son, lest he be angry, and you perish in the way, for his wrath is quickly kindled. Blessed are all who take refuge in him.*

Kiss the Son, that is, pay homage to Jesus the Son while you still have time.

9
What God Delights In
(6:4-6)

Here God states what gives Him delight. Verse 6 says, *For I desire steadfast love and not sacrifice, the knowledge of God rather than burnt offerings.* This is a major issue in Hosea. God's name is upon them, but they're not living in a way consistent with His name because they don't know Him. Remember what Hosea has already said.

Hosea 5:4 *Their deeds do not permit them to return to their God. For the spirit of whoredom is within them, and they know not the LORD.*

Hosea 4:1 *Listen to the word of the LORD, O sons of Israel, for the LORD has a case against the inhabitants of the land because there is no faithfulness or kindness, or knowledge of God in the land.*

You can't live in a way consistent with the character of God if you don't really know who He is. In the Ten Commandments, notice the word "take."

Exodus 20:7 *You shall not take the name of the LORD your God in vain for the LORD will not hold him guiltless who takes His name in vain.*

Take (תִשָּׂא ṭiś-śā) literally means to lift or carry, rendering this, *you shall not lift or carry the name of Yahweh in emptiness.* The idea is that His name is upon this people, and they are to live in a way that will not evacuate His name of meaning, making His name empty. This certainly includes their speech, but it includes much more.

As we go through life with His name upon us, we should not live in a way that makes God's name meaningless to this world. In us, the world should encounter His true character. Even some believers live in a way inconsistent with their calling. They find that what is true and right seems strange because they do not really know their God. The question is: Do we know Him, really know Him?

WHAT THE PEOPLE HAVE BEEN (6:4)

The Lord begins with a question for the northern and southern kingdoms. *What shall I do with you, O Ephraim? What shall I do with you, O Judah?* Throughout this book, Hosea addresses himself primarily to the northern kingdom, but Judah is not far from his mind because they will also receive judgment if they follow in the footsteps of the northern kingdom. Judgment will come because they've been stubborn and unrepentant.

The Lord's Question

God's question is one that we can relate to since we have used words like these. He is putting things this way so we are able to fully understand that the judgments coming upon the people have been brought upon them by themselves. This question reveals

- A conflict in desires—God does not delight in the death of the wicked. He would rather they repent and live.
- A duty that cannot be ignored—Since He is a God of justice, He must punish sin.
- Efforts that have been ignored—He has reached out to them over and over again.
- The people's full responsibility—they have not left God with any other option.

The People's Pattern (6:4)

The Issue Focused on By God

The lack of covenant faithfulness (חֶסֶד hesed) is God's issue with His people. Their covenant love and loyalty has been like a morning cloud, like the dew that goes early away. Read Chapter 4 to see God's charges against them. Here God is talking about the commitment that ought to be present when there is a right relationship with Him, the kind of loyalty that ought to be present in a covenant relationship.

They've chosen sin instead of covenant loyalty to God. Where sin abounds, covenant loyalty goes away. Loyalty between family members disappears—between parents and children and between spouses. This is a sign of a wicked people. When a society descends into the cesspool of sin, the presence of God's kind of love and loyalty disappears.

True love and loyalty are, deep within, an unselfish commitment to God. Sin, on the other hand, is not about God. It is about the lie that there is something more valuable, more trustworthy and more satisfying than God. Sin is selfish, putting self at the center. Sin is a fundamentally disloyal act against God.

A cautionary note: Loyalty to family members must never be placed above loyalty to God and to all He represents. When there is a family member who is in sin, you must stand on the side of truth with that person. This is the most loyal thing you could do for him. You are disloyal to God and to him if you do anything else.

The Point Where the People Have Sinned

As individuals they have been unfaithful to God, as well as to His law, His desires, His people, and His interests. Their self-proclaimed faithfulness and love for God are like a morning cloud or the morning mist, fickle and temporary. Their commitment to God is only until anything else comes along that they want, which equals no commitment at all. They have been unfaithful, with no covenant loyalty.

WHAT THE LORD HAS DONE (6:5)

Confrontation

God has confronted Israel with His *words* and through His *prophets*. This confrontation has been:

- Pointed—He has described their sin in unmistakable terms. They will never have to wonder what God has seen.
- Powerful—God has pronounced their death. Through His prophets, the Word of God has come to them and said, "If you don't repent, you're going to die."
- Personal—God has spoken to them through the prophets, face-to-face, so that they see real, living, breathing human beings standing

in front of them with the words of God in their mouths, telling them what will happen if they don't repent.

All of this has been an expression of God's faithfulness. He could have judged the people without any confrontation whatsoever, and not given them any warning. God did not owe them one, or space, time, and an opportunity to repent, but in verses 4-5 He even pleads with them saying, *"What shall I do with you, O Ephraim? What shall I do with you, O Judah? I have hewn them by the prophets; I have slain them by the words of my mouth,..."* It was God's love and His faithful nature which warned and confronted.

NOTE: Love does confront, and not in such fluffy terms that no one knows they're being confronted. If we look at God's example, He confronts them in terms that are unmistakable and in terms that communicate the gravity of the situation. Faithful, godly confrontation is love. Any love that is vague and doesn't call for repentance, is a love different from God's love. If people are headed for destruction and we love them, we had better communicate their true situation to them in terms that reflect that they are really headed for destruction. Humbly, yes, lovingly, yes, but unmistakably.

WHY GOD HAS DONE IT (6:6)

God has judged His people because of Who He is. He's confronted them because of what He desires. If you really know God, then know this: He doesn't want mere sacrifice. God never intended that those sacrifices in the Old Testament be apart from faith. They were to be offered in true faith toward God. If you tried to substitute sacrifice for faith, it was abominable and hateful to Him. What is absent in the life of the nation is precisely what God has said He desires.

APPLYING IT

Are you trying to substitute something for commitment and loyalty to God? He wants your covenant loyalty—not your sacrifice, not your "whole burnt offerings." He wants your heart. Are you trying to buy God off? Are you trying to substitute things like these?

- Worship attendance
- Giving
- A Christian compartment in your life
- Biblical rationalizations for your sins

- Self-judgment that stops short of repentance—"I know I'm doing wrong, but at least I'm better than those hypocrites, because at least I acknowledge that I ... ."

If you've been disloyal to God, to His Word, to His people, to your commitments, and now suddenly start being loyal and faithful, what will change in your life? What will your return look like?

We are all hopelessly, helplessly covenant-breakers from birth. If you'll turn from your sins to trust in God's Son, the Bible says He will forgive all your sins and by His grace, receive you to Himself as His own child. God will change your nature and your heart, making you a person who keeps covenant and delights the Lord.

10

What God Hates

(6:7-11)

God's issue with Israel is their covenant unfaithfulness. In verses 4-6 of chapter 6, He tells what delights Him: *steadfast love and not sacrifice, the knowledge of God rather than burnt offerings.* The indictment switches beginning with verse 7, emphasizing what He hates. God reveals His knowledge of their sin and tells them specifically what calls out to Him for their judgment. His revelation is His gracious warning to them.

COVENANT BREAKERS (6:7)

God hates the fact that they transgress the covenant and says you can trace this covenant-breaking all the way back to the first man. There has been a lot of discussion about how verse 7 should be translated and understood. Did they break the covenant *at Adam, like men,* or *like Adam?* Some understand Adam to be the name for a place. (Joshua 3:16 mentions a city named Adam.) Rendering it that way requires a questionable understanding of the preposition. It is understood to mean "like, as, according to," not "at." Others take Adam to simply refer to *men,* since the word Adam does mean man. But it makes perfect sense to translate it *like Adam,* as do the New American Standard and the English Standard versions. God is saying that Israel has acted toward God just like the first man, as Adam did back in the garden. In his act of rebellion, Israel can see their act of rebellion. Adam transgressed the covenant that God made with him. God gave Adam blessings and responsibility, but he proved unfaithful to that charge. We don't know everything that God communicated to Adam, but we know enough from Genesis to know these things—

God dealt bountifully with Adam.

He gave Adam:

- Life.
- Honor and responsibility—made him the ruler over the earth in the early days when the animals were brought before him and he gave them names, indicating his headship over creation.
- A helper fit for him—someone to live beside in a life of worship to God.
- A gracious boundary—Adam's one prohibition served as a reminder that his Creator was and is God. It reminded him that even though he was given authority over creation, it was delegated, and he ruled under the authority of God.

Adam dealt with God unfaithfully.

Adam's answer to all that goodness was to transgress his covenant relationship with God. God was faithful; Adam was unfaithful. God is a covenant-keeper; Adam was a covenant-breaker. Israel's unfaithfulness is captured in the picture of Adam's sin in the garden.

The people of God have followed the pattern.

This is the history of man from the beginning of time, and sadly, this is the pattern with the children of Israel. Each time it has five stages:

1. Gracious blessing
2. Unfaithfulness to God
3. Judgment
4. Pleas for mercy
5. Deliverance

The whole pattern then repeats over and over again in the Old Testament. Maybe they have presumed that the pattern will continue forever, or maybe they don't believe God will judge them and leave them broken beyond remedy.

God still hates covenant-breaking, and He still hates the absence of covenant faithfulness. Are you faithful to God, His Word and His ways, or do you fit that pattern of covenant-breaking? Has your love for God proven to be fickle? Could the charge against Job, which proved to be false, be true in your own case?

Job 1:9 *Then Satan answered the* LORD *and said, "Does Job fear God for no reason?* *¹⁰ Have you not put a hedge around him and his house and all that he has, on every side? You have blessed the work of his hands, and his possessions have increased in the land. ¹¹ But stretch out your hand and touch all that he has, and he will curse you to your face."*

God hates covenant-breaking.

Isaiah 33:8 *The highways lie waste; the traveler ceases. Covenants are broken; cities are despised; there is no regard for man.*

Isa 24:5 *The earth is also polluted by its inhabitants, for they transgressed laws, violated statutes, broke the everlasting covenant.*

Malachi 2:13 *And this second thing you do. You cover the* LORD'*s altar with tears, with weeping and groaning because he no longer regards the offering or accepts it with favor from your hand. ¹⁴ But you say, "Why does he not?" Because the* LORD *was witness between you and the wife of your youth, to whom you have been faithless, though she is your companion and your wife by covenant.*

PRODUCERS OF EVIL (6:8)

Gilead here may refer to a city, Ramoth-Gilead, east of the Jordan River, or another city called Jabesh-Gilead. It may be a reference to the entire region east of the Jordan River, the region being so united in its wickedness and its rebellion toward God that it's like one city.

We don't know why God singles it out. Maybe some specific atrocity occurred there that these people would be familiar with, or maybe this is an example of a people united in sin. We can be certain, though, that a constant pattern of violent injustice characterizes the land at that time.

The phrase *city of evil doers* literally means *workers of wickedness* or *makers of wickedness*. According to a NET Bible note, "The Hebrew here is an ironic play on the professional occupation function (see *IBHS* 615 §37.2c)."[11] In

---

[11] *IBHS* is *An Introduction to Biblical Hebrew Syntax* by B. Waltke and M. O'Connor (Eisenbrauns, 1990).

effect, the major "professional guild" in Gilead is evil-working; the people are producers of evil!

As a nation moves deeper and deeper into sin, that which used to insult our senses becomes increasingly commonplace, and insanity becomes the norm. Injustices that once would have caused outrage have now come to be expected. Right and wrong are reversed. God hates a society that is cruel, heartless, and without compassion or a conscience. He hates the production of evil.

Hos 4:2 *There is swearing, deception, murder, stealing, and adultery. They employ violence, so that bloodshed follows bloodshed.*

Romans 1:30 *slanderers, haters of God, insolent, arrogant, boastful, inventors of evil, disobedient to parents*

CONSPIRATORS IN CRIME (6:9)

There are a couple of views that describe this activity.

John Gill, the old pastor who was a predecessor of Spurgeon:

> ... as good people passed by Gilead to Shechem, and so to Jerusalem, to worship there at the solemn feasts, they lay in wait for them, and murdered them; because they did not give into the idolatrous worship of the calves at Dan and Bethel ....

Keil and Delitzsch commentary:

> The way to Sichem is mentioned as a place of murders and bloody deeds, because the road from Samaria the capital, and in fact from the northern part of the kingdom generally, to Bethel the principal place of worship belonging to the kingdom of the ten tribes, lay through this city. Pilgrims to the feasts for the most part took this road; and the priests, who were taken from the dregs of the people, appear to have lain in wait for them, either to rob, or, in case of resistance, to murder.

Surely they have committed <u>crime</u> (New American Standard) or *villainy* (English Standard). One source says it can refer to unnatural crimes, but what is certain is that their evil has been planned, entered into willingly, without any fear of the judgment of God. These are their so-called priests!

Israel has set up its own mock religious system. Their priests are not from the tribe of Levi, but from the dregs of the people, and they have turned into a band of robbers. They have their own false gods and feasts (see 1 Kings 12:25-33). These priests take these days of celebration and worship to be their opportunity to lie in wait and to rob the pilgrims as they make their way to Bethel.

When people conspire in sin, they have reached a new place of disregard for God. He sees, knows and cares when you plan together to dishonor His name.

HORRIBLE DEFILEMENT (6:10)

It is unclear, given the imagery used elsewhere in this book, whether this is literal *whoredom* or spiritual whoredom. Instead of trusting God and obeying His laws, Israel has looked to its own ways and to foreign alliances. There is spiritual whoredom because idolatry is being practiced in the land. It is also true that the worship of the Baals involves cultic prostitution. There is no proper house of worship in Israel, so the idea here is not a temple. Rather, the entire nation is characterized by this *horrible* defiling sin. Not only is this sin horrible, but it has spread to all Israel, becoming pervasive. A people are in a horrible condition when they glory in their shame and they don't blush at what is defiling behavior. God is holy. He hates impurity and says, *You shall therefore be holy, for I am holy* (Lev. 11.45).

This impurity is not the standard for God's people. The horrible sins of today should be abhorrent to us, the people who wear His name.

SOWING FOR JUDGMENT (6:11)

God, through Hosea, has a warning for Judah too, but the warning describes the sinning of Israel as a harvest of judgment since they both have sown seeds of destruction. He makes this point even while He states that there is reward as well as judgment. For those who believe God and give heed to Him, there will be a day of restored fortunes. However, for those who continue in their disregard for God, proving themselves to be among those who pursue what God hates, there is coming a harvest day, and it won't be a day of joy.

God hates:
- Covenant-breaking
- Production of evil

- Conspiring for crime
- Spiritual and sexual defilement
- Sowing for judgment

Are you living a life that delights in the Lord or one that He despises? Are you daring God to demonstrate His commitment to what delights Him by judging you for your disobedience?

11
Life on the Brink
(7:1-16)

The book of Hosea is the living picture of a people on a foolish course leading them to the brink of destruction. It not only speaks about a nation, but the same course can be seen in an individual who is on the brink of disaster.

This picture can be encouraging, in two ways. For one, if you're not headed toward spiritual destruction, you can be thankful that by the grace of God, your heart has been changed. For another, you can be warned to watch over your heart, to keep it from a foolish course that would lead you to destruction.

In chapter 7, God, through Hosea, uses vivid, memorable comparisons to picture the foolishness and effects of Israel's sins, both on the home front and in its foreign policy. It is important to understand that when you choose sin instead of God, you not only lose sound practice, you also lose sound judgment. One of the ways God judges a people is to systematically take away their ability to make sound choices. The only way we have sound judgment in any area of our lives is by the grace of God.

ON THE BRINK AT HOME (7:1-10)

The heaviest weight: God's willingness to heal (7:1)

The heaviest weight upon the northern kingdom is not God's impending judgment, but His willingness to be gracious by healing them. God has sent His prophets, not only with warning about judgment, but also with the promise of healing if they would repent. So, God has given Israel both time to repent and prophets to deliver His message of judgement. Do you recognize the weightiness of God's goodness? When God's gracious overtures have been ignored, and someone has continued in the stubbornness of their sin, it will testify against them in the coming days. How will someone feel on Judgment Day when they are shown the many opportunities God has given them to repent, but that time after time they chose their sin in stubborn pride?

Revelation 2:20 *But I have this against you, that you tolerate that woman Jezebel, who calls herself a prophetess and is teaching and seducing my servants to practice sexual immorality and to eat food sacrificed to idols. 21 I gave her time to repent, but she refuses to repent of her sexual immorality. 22 Behold, I will throw her onto a sickbed, and those who commit adultery with her I will throw into great tribulation, unless they repent of her works, 23 and I will strike her children dead. And all the churches will know that I am he who searches mind and heart, and I will give to each of you according to your works.*

God's grace has only revealed more sin

God is willing to heal Israel, but He has seen their wickedness. They have incriminated themselves by their unwillingness to listen to the Word of God and their unwillingness to repent. Do you recognize the weightiness of God's goodness in your life? Have you repented, or do you continue to choose sin in your stubborn pride?

Isaiah 3:8 *For Jerusalem has stumbled, and Judah has fallen, because their speech and their deeds are against the LORD, defying his glorious presence. 9 For the look on their faces bears witness against them; they proclaim their sin like Sodom; they do not hide it. Woe to them! For they have brought evil on themselves. 10 Tell the righteous that it shall be well with them, for they shall eat the fruit of their deeds.*

Sins specified (7:1-4)

God doesn't leave them wondering whether He knows their specific sins. He points them out.

1. Deception – All kinds, not just outright lies by speech, but dishonesty and deception in other ways as well.
2. Lawlessness – Thieves breaking in and bandits waiting outside.
3. Irreverence – They do not stop to consider that all of their behavior, motives, words and deeds are before the Lord. They cannot hide from Him.

4. Corruption – Some of their sins are apparently committed while striving to please their kings and princes. Although they are man-pleasers instead of God-pleasers, the real issue is that they are self-pleasers. They engage in corruption to advance themselves.

John 19:14 *Now it was the day of Preparation of the Passover. It was about the sixth hour. He said to the Jews, "Behold your King!" 15 They cried out, "Away with him, away with him, crucify him!" Pilate said to them, "Shall I crucify your King?" The chief priests answered, "We have no king but Caesar."*

Sinful self-seeking can make fast friends, and often it unites in the face of righteousness. Notice the relationship between Herod and Pilate.

Luke 23:8 *When Herod saw Jesus, he was very glad, for he had long desired to see him, because he had heard about him, and he was hoping to see some sign done by him. 9 So he questioned him at some length, but he made no answer. 10 The chief priests and the scribes stood by, vehemently accusing him. 11 And Herod with his soldiers treated him with contempt and mocked him. Then, arraying him in splendid clothing, he sent him back to Pilate. 12 And Herod and Pilate became friends with each other that very day, for before this they had been at enmity with each other.*

Jesus unites people, either in righteousness or in their sin. People don't stand neutral when it come to the Lord Jesus.

5. Adultery – This sin is singled out as characterizing the entire nation. It is true that it may be spiritual unfaithfulness that is most in view here, but it is also true that sexual immorality characterized the people at this time.

Sins Depicted Through Comparison (7:4-10)

God gives them four analogies so they can understand His charges clearly.

Like an oven burning for their unfaithfulness (7:4)

The custom is to prepare dough in the evening and then bake it in the morning after the dough has time to rise. The picture is of an oven that doesn't need to be stoked during the night, because it stays so hot that it will be ready to bake bread in the morning. That is, you don't have to stir these people to evil, to their adultery, spiritual or literal. They are ready.

Proverbs 1:11 *If they say, "Come with us, let us lie in wait for blood; let us ambush the innocent without reason;* [12] *like Sheol let us swallow them alive, and whole, like those who go down to the pit;* [13] *we shall find all precious goods, we shall fill our houses with plunder;* [14] *throw in your lot among us; we will all have one purse"--* [15] *my son, do not walk in the way with them; hold back your foot from their paths,* [16] *for their feet run to evil, and they make haste to shed blood.*

Proverbs 6:16 *There are six things that the LORD hates, seven that are an abomination to him:* [17] *haughty eyes, a lying tongue, and hands that shed innocent blood,* [18] *a heart that devises wicked plans, feet that make haste to run to evil,* [19] *a false witness who breathes out lies, and one who sows discord among brothers.*

Isaiah 59:1 *Behold, the LORD's hand is not shortened, that it cannot save, or his ear dull, that it cannot hear;* [2] *but your iniquities have made a separation between you and your God, and your sins have hidden his face from you so that he does not hear.* [3] *For your hands are defiled with blood and your fingers with iniquity; your lips have spoken lies; your tongue mutters wickedness.* [4] *No one enters suit justly; no one goes to law honestly; they rely on empty pleas, they speak lies, they conceive mischief and give birth to iniquity.* [5] *They hatch adders' eggs; they weave the spider's web; he who eats their eggs dies, and from one that is crushed a viper is hatched.* [6] *Their webs will not serve as clothing; men will not cover themselves with what they make. Their works are works of iniquity, and deeds of violence are in their hands.* [7] *Their feet run to evil, and they are swift to shed innocent blood; their thoughts are thoughts of iniquity; desolation and destruction are in their highways.*

Like an oven burning for their destructive plans (7:5-7)

Now God becomes more specific about this burning-hot oven. Hosea sets a scene before the people. The king is at some celebration, and he does not know that those at the table with him cannot wait to see him assassinated. In fact, 4 of the last 6 kings of the northern kingdom were assassinated.

Instead of the peace and the order and the mutual support that would be present where God is being sought, there is murder, intrigue, deception, self-promotion and sinful alliances. He traces their behavior to its source. They don't seek Him. When men strive, lie in wait, plan and scheme in deceptive ways, they make plain that their hope is not in God.

Like a half-baked cake (7:8)

They are like a cake that is overcooked on one side and still liquid on the other, good for nothing. This is what has become of Israel as they have willingly mixed themselves with the nations. They have adopted foreign gods and pagan practices, and they have taken unbelieving wives. They no longer are a unique people separated unto the Lord, but just like the nations, no good to anyone. For the church or an individual to be spiritually effective, there must be separation unto the Lord.

Like an old man unaware of his weakened condition (7:9-10)

Israel is in its late stages of life, about to be destroyed, but they don't see it. Its strength is given away by compromise and mixing with pagans. This also probably refers to the deals they would make for foreign protection.

At the root of it all

Why do people not listen to God? Why do they refuse to take biblical steps of repentance? Why do they justify themselves in their sin, despite God's specific warnings? Pride. Pride is at the root of all of Israel's stubbornness in listening to God and His Word. They won't humble themselves, therefore their guilt is on their face in their prideful stance. Despite all God's specific warnings, they still refuse to return to Him.

G. Campbell Morgan wrote:

> Signs of decadence, which are patent to others, are undiscovered
> by ourselves; and we go on, and on, and on, the victims of ebbing
> strength, spiritually, and morally becoming degenerate without
> knowing it! We are blind to the signs which are self-evident to
> onlookers. There is no condition more perilous to our highest well-
> being than this of unconscious decadence.[12]

The only hope for a sinful person or a sinful nation is God's grace. Israel is fully responsible, as these chapters make clear, but the ultimate answer for them is a new covenant promise that God has sworn by Himself to bring into existence. When that day comes, He will remove their heart of stone and give them a heart of flesh. If God doesn't choose, in his sovereign grace, to change a heart, how much punishment would it take to turn them? The answer is that there isn't enough.

WITHOUT SOUND JUDGMENT TOWARD THE NATIONS (7:11-12)

One of the ways that sin judges a person or a people is that it takes away sound judgment. Wisdom comes from the Lord. An accurate view of life,

---

[12] Cited by James Montgomery Boice, *Minor Prophets*, pg.53

and the ideas necessary to navigate it, comes from God. When a people or an individual begins to think in a way contrary to Scripture, they forfeit sound judgment. Sound judgment always agrees with Scripture.

The lack of sound thinking and judgment is expressed not only in the realm of behavior, but also in the realm of decisions regarding others. In the life of a nation, it isn't just the domestic front that reveals the effects of sin; it is foreign policy also. Verses 11-16 reveal three expressions of Israel's lack of sound judgment. We also learn its effect in the life of an individual.

The Reason for the Analogy (7:11)

Israel is compared to a dove as it flitters from one thing to another. This is the foreign policy of the northern kingdom. They don't trust in their God, nor look to Him for their safety. By looking out for themselves through shrewd and deceptive agreements, Israel was really on a course that would seal their fate. Motivated by fear, being fickle and naïve, they have entered into one agreement after another, and some conflict with one another.

Robert Chisholm Jr. in his commentary on Hosea talks about this comparison.

In her efforts to arrange foreign alliances, Israel could be compared to a dove, which exhibits little sense... Under Menahem (743 or 738 B.C.) Israel submitted to Assyrian suzerainty (2 Kings 15:19-20). Pekah (734 B.C.) joined a coalition against Assyria, which Tiglath-Pileser III violently crushed (2 Kings 15:29). Hoshea (ca. 732-722 B.C.) after acknowledging Assyrian rulership for a time, stopped tribute payments and sought an alliance with Egypt (2 Kings 17:3-4a). This act of rebellion led to the destruction of the northern kingdom (2 Kings 17:4b-6), the inevitable result of a foreign policy which for 20 years had been characterized by vacillating and expedient measures.[13]

The Result of Their Behavior (7:12)

Staying with the analogy of a dove, God says that the result of this is that HE, the Lord, will be like a fowler, like a bird catcher. He is going to bring the northern kingdom down by the Assyrians, so that when the Assyrians act, it will picture the net of God. He judges by working through the

---

[13] The Bible Knowledge Commentary Old Testament, pg.1395

unsound judgments of those who have refused and rejected Him. They make choices that ultimately lead to their devastation. Whatever is happening in the realm of world affairs is the result of God's work, not just by chance.

Read 1 Kings 22:6-38 to see an example of God's work in the circumstances of the death of Ahab, King of Israel. Here, Ahab had already heard the prophecy of his death from the prophet, Elijah.

1 Kings 21:19 *And you shall speak to him, saying, "Thus says the LORD, 'Have you murdered, and also taken possession?'" And you shall speak to him, saying, "Thus says the LORD, 'In the place where the dogs licked up the blood of Naboth the dogs shall lick up your blood, even yours.'"*

WITHOUT SOUND JUDGMENT TOWARD GOD (7:13-14)

Woe is declared on Israel because she has strayed from God. The word translated *strayed* means to flee. In fact, some translations have it this way: *They have fled from me.* This is very abrupt and straight to the point in the Hebrew text. Instead of running to God, they have run from Him.

Their rebellion will lead to their destruction. Over and over in Hosea, it's stressed that this is due not only to their sins, but their lack of knowledge. Instead of submitting to God, they have rebelled against Him. If they knew the Lord, they would honor and believe Him. Instead, they lie about and against Him by speaking all kinds of words that are contrary to the truth about Him, and what it means to truly follow Him.

Besides straying, rebelling and lying, *they cry and they wail*, but it's not God that they want. It's *grain and wine* (7:14). They desire His benefits, not Him. Instead of rending their heart, they tear their flesh. There's no real brokenness. In keeping with the cultic behavior of Baal worship, they're gashing themselves, trying to get the attention of the gods.

This same message is in the Book of Joel.

Joel 2:12 *"Yet even now," declares the LORD, "return to me with all your heart, with fasting, with weeping, and with mourning;* [13] *and rend your hearts and not your garments." Return to the LORD your God, for he is gracious and merciful, slow to anger, and abounding in steadfast love; and he relents over disaster.*

The common sign among Israelites for mourning over sin was to wear sackcloth and ashes and to rend their garments. God does not want torn garments, but torn hearts. God goes on to say through Joel that He will relent, if they repent. Jonah knew this also, regarding the Ninevites.

In I Kings 18:25-29 we see the Israelites cutting themselves with swords and lances until the blood gushed out, to get the attention of Baal. They're looking for help, but don't go to God on His terms. They bring everything except a broken heart.

1 Kings 18:25 *Then Elijah said to the prophets of Baal, "Choose for yourselves one bull and prepare it first, for you are many, and call upon the name of your god, but put no fire to it." 26 And they took the bull that was given them, and they prepared it and called upon the name of Baal from morning until noon, saying, "O Baal, answer us!" But there was no voice, and no one answered. And they limped around the altar that they had made. 27 And at noon Elijah mocked them, saying, "Cry aloud, for he is a god. Either he is musing, or he is relieving himself, or he is on a journey, or perhaps he is asleep and must be awakened." 28 And they cried aloud and cut themselves after their custom with swords and lances, until the blood gushed out upon them. 29 And as midday passed, they raved on until the time of the offering of the oblation, but there was no voice. No one answered; no one paid attention.*

The most deranged behavior exhibited in sin is the sinner's abhorrence of God. The sinner runs from his only refuge and refuses the only One who can satisfy his soul. Running from God is evidenced by running from His appointed means. You run from:

- His people, the church.
- The sound preaching and teaching of His word.
- The correction and discipline that would restore you to right fellowship.

The irony is, however, that the sinner often seeks help. This is the great deception of sin that is revealed in the unsound judgment of the sinner. The sinner congratulates himself with the idea that he is not avoiding his problems. He is seeking help. The truth, however, is that it's help on his own terms, not God's terms. As a result, it is help that is no help. Any so-called help that refuses God's terms is no help at all in the end.

WITHOUT SOUND JUDGMENT CONCERNING DIRECTION (7:15-16)

Against the Goodness of God (7:15)

He has done good to them, but they have done evil to Him.

Proverbs 17:13 *If anyone returns evil for good, evil will not depart from his house.*

Against the Discipline of God (7:16)

The discipline has come from heaven. Israel feels its effects, but they don't turn upward toward God. In response to God's discipline they begin to look for their answers on a horizontal plane, but the problem is vertical.

Against the Help of God (7:16)

Israel is like a warped bow that sends its arrows astray. It's no good in battle. The Lord has selected them like a bow to send arrows of truth against the idolatry of all the rest of the nations, but they have used his blessing to honor the idols that they were meant to destroy. In a sense, that's what all sinning Christians do. They are like a useless and dangerous weapon.

They have trusted in an untrustworthy defense, looking now to Egypt, now to Assyria. What they think will be their safety will turn out to be their destruction. They have been deceived.

Instead of returning to the Lord with humble, broken, sorrowful speech which would be appropriate (see 14:1-2), their speech reveals insolence, indignation (anger), and pride (literally, "defiance of their tongue").

They don't respond rightly to the message of Hosea or any other prophet, and that is why they will ultimately be destroyed by the Assyrians. They are going back into *Egypt*. He's using Egypt in a figurative sense, reminding Israel of its bondage to Egypt and their deliverance. Instead of being delivered **from Egypt by faith** in the God who would redeem them, they will be delivered **to Egypt** (spiritually speaking – Assyria), due to their **lack of faith in God**.

APPLYING IT

We have seen that where an individual or where a nation pursues sin instead of submitting to God, one of the ways they are judged is they lose sound judgment. They are deranged in sin, losing their senses. What's the answer for that? Remember Jesus' parable of the prodigal son (Luke 15:11-24). *When he came to himself*—that is, when he came to his senses—he realized that his father's servants had enough food, while he himself was starving. He decided to go back to his father and to ask to be treated as one of the servants. When he comes to his senses, he sees his sin for what it is, blaming nobody but himself. He takes full responsibility for it, realizing that he deserves nothing. Then he goes to his father hoping for some slight mercy. Instead, the son meets with a father who's willing, more willing than he ever imagined, to have him back alive.

If your thinking has been deranged by your sin, you are headed in a way that will ultimately lead to your destruction. Instead of running from God, you need to come to your senses and run to the Lord by looking to His Son.

And if you know someone who is out of their mind, who has fled from the Lord, stop treating them as if they're making sense. Lovingly, gently point them to the only true solution for their problem. And pray that they would run to the Lord. We may be an instrument, but only the Lord can bring someone to a right mind.

2 Timothy 2:24 *And the Lord's servant must not be quarrelsome but kind to everyone, able to teach, patiently enduring evil, 25 correcting his opponents with gentleness. God may perhaps grant them repentance leading to a knowledge of the truth, 26 and they may come to their senses and escape from the snare of the devil, after being captured by him to do his will.*

12
Sowing Wind, Reaping Whirlwind
(8:1-14)

Warning is a gracious thing. But in the lives of rebellious people, it isn't viewed as gracious, nor is it received graciously. We don't like being warned if our heart is in a rebellious state. How the warning is viewed, and how it is received, doesn't change the fact that it is indeed an act of grace.

God doesn't owe a warning to anyone. He could bring judgment that's immediate, devastating and final without ever warning anyone, and He would owe no one an apology. Every moment of time that God gives for repentance, and every time He raises His voice to say, "You'd better turn! You'd better repent!"—every time He does that, it's grace.

TWO PROVERBIAL STATEMENTS, 8:7

The northern kingdom, as we've seen, is on its deathbed due to its own sin, yet God is still warning. Two of His warnings stand in the center of this chapter in the form of proverbial statements.

They Sow the Wind and Reap the Whirlwind.

8:7 *For they sow the wind,*
  and they shall reap the whirlwind.

That is God's proverbial way of warning both them and us that sin's effects are multiplied. What we think to be a small act of sowing turns out to be a major act toward our undoing.

You cannot control sin while you choose it. You cannot get sin to behave. What you sow in small measure (or so you think), returns upon you in large measure.

They sow vanity, and they shall reap a harvest of destruction. They sow sin, and they shall reap trouble.

Have you learned that? Have you learned, yet, that sin is so dangerous and so deadly, that you should refuse it and stand against it, even as it offers itself to you in small measures? Those so-called small compromises eventually lead to large failures and devastating consequences, so we should fear sin even in its germ state, even in its smallest state.

As someone has said, "Sin will take you farther than you wanted to go, keep you longer than you wanted to stay and cost you more than you wanted to pay."

The standing grain has no heads; it shall yield no flour.

There's no doubt a literal element to this. We've already seen—and will see it again in this chapter and in the 9th chapter—how one of the ways that God judges the people is to progressively take away provision, removing blessing. The rebellious nation will end up with drought and famine. Not only is it true to say that sin is <u>destructive</u>. We can also turn it around and say that there is <u>nothing productive</u> in sin. You don't get something productive (flour) where there is no fruit (no heads of grain). There is no fruit for God, fruit for life. Israel is living in a state that's fruitless, so there's nothing profitable in the people. There is nothing good, nothing ultimately satisfying in sin. That pathway is absolutely unproductive. When you choose it and pursue it, you wake up one day and discover that all you have to show for the choices you have made is the whirlwind of self-destruction. And yet, while the germ of destruction is in every act of sin, sin simply doesn't simply operate on its own. God is at work in the whirlwind. He set the moral laws of the universe in place, and He visits sin with judgment. When you choose sin, you set yourself in opposition to God.

Now, let's go back and look at the other verses of this chapter.

THE REALITY OF IMPENDING JUDGMENT (8:1a)

God says to *set the trumpet to your lips,* alerting the community to danger.

One like a vulture (ESV) or *an eagle* (NASB) is about to descend upon the house of the Lord (the land of the northern kingdom). Most believe this refers to the griffon vulture, a common bird in Old Testament Israel. It's known to be where there are battlefields and dead bodies. This majestic scavenger bird is hovering over the land. Why? Because very soon there will be death and destruction. The vulture in this case is Assyria, the nation that will conquer them. They are on the verge of judgment. They deserve it. But God in His grace is still warning. *Set a trumpet to your lips,* because if they'll listen, there's still space for repentance. Remember in chapter 7, *When I would have healed Israel ....* The Lord is ready to heal them, but they won't listen.

THE REASON FOR IMPENDING JUDGMENT (8:1b)

Why is this bird hovering over the land, ready to devour them? Because of their sin. He explains sin in two ways here: The transgression of a covenant and rebellion against law. Both make up what sin is. Yet in the minds of many professing believers today, these two things are not connected.

It Is Personal Transgression

God says, *they have transgressed my covenant.* A covenant is essentially personal. It is an agreement between two parties. The people of Israel have *transgressed* or *passed over;* they have violated their covenant with God. As we have seen before, they are covenant-breakers, and God hates covenant-breaking.

Sin is always personal. It is <u>against God.</u> Look at how personal this is to Him:

> *My* covenant (8:1)
> *My* law (8:1)
> To *me* they cry (8:2)
> Not through *me* (8:4)
> *I* knew it not (8:4)
> *I* have spurned your calf, O Samaria (8:5)
> *My* anger burns (8:5)

And on it goes. This entire chapter makes plain that sin is a personal affront to God. When you sin, you are acting against God. There is personal interaction between God and the nation. He's saying, in essence, "You have sinned against Me; therefore, this is what I am going to do."

It is precise rebellion (8:1)

Sin is not just general. It is not some vague, unidentifiable thing. God says to them, you have rebelled against my law, against my instruction. In fact, he will say later (8:12) that even though He has made His will specifically and unmistakably known, they act as if they have no knowledge of it. Sin is not defined by your feelings. People may say, "Well, I just don't feel like I'm wrong," or "I just don't see it that way," or "I just don't think about it that way." But that's not the end of the matter. People think they can define what sin is, but men don't define sin. God defines sin. Sin is relational, but it's not just relational. It is when you transgress, violate, ignore, reject or rebel against what God has specified to be contrary to His will. God has given us His will, and it is found in His Word. When we act, think, speak and feel in a way that is contrary to the Word of God, that is sin.

What has Israel done? They have transgressed a covenant. That's relational, sinning against God. And how have they done it? *They have rebelled against My law.* And, by the way, they are absolutely without excuse, as God magnifies in verse 12. *Were I to write for him my laws by the ten thousands, they would be regarded as a strange thing.* The Lord has made His law known to them in a way that is absolutely sufficient, but they are still strangers to it. They act as if they've never seen it or heard it. He's told them the truth, but they ignore it and rebel against it. That is sin.

Today, many people are acting in a defiant, rebellious way toward the clear teaching of Scripture, but imagine that they have their own self-defined relationship with God and are fine. They will say, "I am pursuing the Lord," while there are glaring areas of disobedience in their life. People who are sinning against the Lord often claim to be seeking Him.

You cannot be right with God personally, while you willingly rebel against His precepts. That's a personal affront to God. To put it another way, just because you don't FEEL any personal animosity toward God, it doesn't mean that your life is not an expression of hatred toward Him.

One evidence of this, as we will see, is one's attitude toward those who bring a message contrary to their current course.

Amos 5:10 *They hate him who reproves in the gate, and they abhor him who speaks the truth.*

THE REVELATIONS OF THEIR REBELLION (8:2-13)

As we see the revelations of their rebellion, we need to examine our own lives. What does rebellion against the Lord look like in the life of an individual or in the life of a nation?

Empty Profession (8:2-3)

Israel has not been denying, either intellectually or verbally, that Yahweh is God. They denied it by action. They deny it by choice. They claim to know Him; they appeal to Him on the basis that they know Him (*To me they cry*, verse 2), and yet the whole time they have been crying out to Him, they have *spurned the good*. They say they know Him, but they don't obey Him. So, God says, *the enemy shall pursue him.*

How? Notice what God is spurning: Their *calf* (8:5). They spurned the good, not only morally, but in terms of their false worship.

The New Testament also declares that it's empty to say that you know the Lord if you're not willing to follow Him. Hear the words of Jesus and of James.

Luke 6:46 *"Why do you call me 'Lord, Lord,' and not do what I tell you?"*

James 2:26 *For as the body apart from the spirit is dead, so also faith apart from works is dead.*

We say we know the Lord, but when He makes known to us what is good, will we follow Him in it, or will we spurn the good? What would reveal that you are on a similar path today? Are your actions a direct and willful contradiction to your profession? Are you spurning, rejecting, turning away from what God has identified as good while relying on what you call a relationship with God?

Presumptuous Actions (8:4)

They are setting up leaders without seeking the Lord's direction. They are engaging in choices that are monumentally important, indeed, choices that are not even rightfully theirs to make apart from God's guidance, and never even seeking His guidance. When God says, *They set up princes, but I knew it not,* we know that He really does know. What He means is that they weren't talking to Him about it. They weren't depending on Him. That's what a rebellious life looks like. It's when someone begins to live as a practical atheist, making decisions but not seeking God's guidance.

This evil isn't only in the Old Testament. It's not just about setting up kings and princes in a theocratic setting. It's about any sort of decision. What kind of presumptuous activity is showing up in the lives of people today? Here are some examples, though not an exhaustive list.

Presumptuous business dealings

James 4:13 *Come now, you who say, "Today or tomorrow we will go into such and such a town and spend a year there and trade and make a profit"—* [14] *yet you do not know what tomorrow will bring. What is your life? For you are a mist that appears for a little time and then vanishes.* [15] *Instead you ought to say, "If the Lord wills, we will live and do this or that."* [16] *As it is, you boast in your arrogance. All such boasting is evil.*

It's not wrong to make plans. It's wrong to make plans not realizing that we are absolutely dependent upon God for what tomorrow will bring. It's to make plans without realizing that our plans must begin with God and must be submitted to Him.

Presumptuous romance

Proverbs 19:14 *House and wealth are inherited from fathers, but a prudent wife is from the Lord.*

Many professing believers presume that they can find someone to love apart from God's guidance, apart from the principles found in Scripture, or in direct defiance of what He has set forth in Scripture. But for the obedient believer, it's not so much about, "God, is this the one?" No, it's more about submitting to God, so we could say, "Lord, You are the love of my life. You are my chief interest, so I'm going to live my life trusting that if Your plan for me is marriage, You will lead someone into my life who has the same priorities." It's not just a matter of finding someone who says they are a Christian. The standard is, "Can I find someone through God's guidance and providence who will serve Him together with me, investing our lives in ministry together?"

Presumptuous planning

Many claim Christ, but totally ignore Him in the management of their time and their money. They run their business or their career by the world's standards, or they invest in what's godless. Then they expect God's blessing in their returns.

Do we seek the Lord's guidance concerning things like choosing a college or choosing a job or taking a business trip?

Some may think that seeking the Lord's will in these things would be hyper-spiritual. "God gives us a brain. We can function on our own. Do we really need the Lord's guidance?" That's what secularism does—it reduces us until we are blind to God's presence and His activity. It reduces us to thinking prayer is ineffectual and unnecessary. That's what rebellion looks like.

Self-Styled Religion (8:4-6)

They took *their silver and gold* that God supplied, but how did they use it?

To offend God

The Lord says, *I have spurned your calf, O Samaria. My anger burns against them.* Remember that Jeroboam originally had calves stationed in Dan and Bethel. When the Lord through Hosea says *your calf, O Samaria,* He's talking about the whole northern kingdom.

We would be wrong to think that they actually worshipped the calves. Archaeology has discovered sketches where Baal is pictured as standing on the calves. The calves are seen as pictures of strength upon which the gods stand. Israel in Hosea's day is still using the name Yahweh, but they have connected Him with the Baals of the pagans. Remember when Aaron followed the people and made a calf.

Exodus 32:4 *And he received the gold from their hand and fashioned it with a graving tool and made a golden calf. And they said, "These are your gods, O Israel, who brought you up out of the land of Egypt!" ⁵When Aaron saw this, he built an altar before it. And Aaron made a proclamation and said, "Tomorrow shall be a feast to the LORD."*

The idea is, "We're going to worship the true God by means of the calf." They are worshipping God in a way that they have imagined. Self-styled religion is idolatry, trying to take the living God Who cannot be pictured in an image, and then to reduce Him to an image. But it's also the consumer mindset in terms of the worship of God. It's worshipping God in my own way, according to my tastes, in a way that's not authorized nor desired by God.

To destroy themselves

They took the silver and gold that the Lord supplied, and they used it to offend him. Notice the end of verse 4, *With their silver and gold they made idols for their own destruction.* When you live an idolatrous life, putting things in the place of God, or when you try to worship God in your own self-styled manner, you are engaging in behavior that will lead to your own destruction.

We do not have the right to worship God any way we wish. Worship is not about us, not for us, not determined by us, not measured by us. It's God-centered, according to what He has revealed.

Stubborn Alliances (8:8-10)

Like a stubborn *wild donkey*, unwilling to be guided, Israel goes looking for help on her own terms. As we saw in chapter 7, they are like a dove flitting back and forth between Assyria and Egypt, breaking one relationship to form the other. Then they break that one to reestablish the first, thinking they are being shrewd. Israel spends their money paying *tribute*, but they are wasting away as a result. They are *swallowed up* by the nations, viewed as a *useless* pot that nobody wants, like a donkey. Donkeys are stubborn and hard to handle. That's how the northern kingdom of Israel is. They want no restraint, no guidance. They don't want to submit to God. Instead, they are *wandering alone*.

When submitted to God, He grants them an honored position, but when rebelling against God, instead of acquiring greater honor, they lose it. The northern kingdom is reduced to a buyer with *hired lovers*, looking for someone she can pay to love her and to care for her in these alliances. But it won't work. God says He *will soon gather them up* for judgment, and they will waste away under an oppressive regime.

How ironic that man, in his sin, would trade the ruling power of God that is benevolent and blesses, for an oppressive rule that will use one up and destroy. That is still the choice that sin makes. Jesus said His yoke is easy and His burden is light. Life in Christ includes joy, peace, fulfillment and satisfaction. But when you say no to the Lord and begin to look to the world for your satisfaction, you end up in an oppressive relationship and become a slave of sin.

Meaningless Sacrifices (8:11-13a)

They have *multiplied altars*, but in doing that, they have multiplied their *sinning*. Why? Because the Lord *does not accept* their sacrifices.

Not sanctioned by God

They are not worshipping God in the way that He directed. Instead of going to the temple in Jerusalem, they have set up altars in Dan and Bethel.

Not sincere

They are violating God's law, yet thinking that their self-styled religion will be acceptable to Him.

The result is multiplied sin

Empty religion is distasteful to the Lord. It just means multiplied sin. When you are sitting in a worship service, you may think you're doing a good thing, but if your heart is not willing to submit to the Lord, your so-called worship is completely unacceptable to Him.

Replacements for God (8:14)

They replace their dependency on God and His power, substituting what they can build with their own hands—palaces and fortified cities. Soon, what they have constructed with their hands will be torn down. This can happen in a church. "Can't you tell we're doing well? Look at the size of our building. Look at the size of our budget. Haven't you seen our programs? Doesn't big mean blessing?" Not if you built it with your own hands. What the church needs more than anything is not bigger anything. We need the Lord. We need His power, His blessing, His favor. We can have the biggest productions the world has ever seen, but if lives are unchanged by the power of God, it's emptiness.

APPLYING IT

Do you realize the deadly nature of sin, even when yielded to in small ways?

Does your life bear the marks of someone who is rebelling against God?

- Empty words
- Presumptuous actions

- Self-styled religion
- Stubborn alliances
- Meaningless sacrifices
- Replacements for God

What's the answer, if this chapter is describing you? The answer is repentance. You respond to the warning of God by turning to Him. He's made a way for rebellious sinners, and His name is Jesus. You may say, "But I already know this Jesus." He said, "Why do you call Me 'Lord, Lord,' and not do what I say?" If you know Him, follow Him.

13
Abandoned by God
(9:1-9)

This 9th chapter depicts the sure judgment and coming devastation to the northern kingdom. God will withdraw His special protective care over them because they have turned to other gods. A chilling statement found in verses 11-12 explains what is coming:

"Ephraim's glory shall fly away like a bird—no birth, no pregnancy, no conception! Even if they bring up children, I will bereave them till none is left." And then God says, "Woe to them when I depart from them!"

This was prophesied back when the Lord commissioned Joshua in the presence of Moses:

Deuteronomy 31:14 *And the LORD said to Moses, "Behold, the days approach when you must die. Call Joshua and present yourselves in the tent of meeting, that I may commission him." And Moses and Joshua went and presented themselves in the tent of meeting. 15 And the LORD appeared in the tent in a pillar of cloud. And the pillar of cloud stood over the entrance of the tent. 16 And the LORD said to Moses, "Behold, you are about to lie down with your fathers. Then this people will rise and whore after the foreign gods among them in the land that they are entering, and they will forsake me and break my covenant that I have made with them. 17 Then my anger will be kindled against them in that day, and I will forsake them and hide my face from them, and they will be devoured. And many evils and troubles will come upon them, so that they will say in that day, 'Have not these evils come upon us because our God is not among us?' 18 And I will surely hide my face in that day because of all the evil that they have done, because they have turned to other gods.*

The omnipresence of God is never escaped, but His presence in terms of favor, fellowship, protection, provision, and in terms of man's senses, can be withdrawn. When people abandon Him for other gods, He then abandons them to the gods they have chosen, the gods that are not gods.

Men often imagine in their sin that they want God to leave them alone. They usually don't say it directly, "God, would You just leave me alone!" Instead, they may shut themselves off from the God-ordained means of their repentance and recovery. They don't want to see or to hear from the people God would use. They don't realize it, but when they turn away from God's ordained means of turning them back from sin, they are actually asking God to leave them alone. It is a terrible thing when God decides to oblige. We saw the idea of being left alone back in chapter 4.

Hosea 4:16 *Like a stubborn heifer, Israel is stubborn; can the* LORD *now feed them like a lamb in a broad pasture?* [17] *Ephraim is joined to idols; leave him alone.*

This is what is depicted in the 9th chapter. God is telling us what will come upon the nation because He is withdrawing. They will be left with what they can provide themselves, and that is nothing—nothing but destruction.

WHAT THEY CAN EXPECT AS GOD DEPARTS (9:1-7)

The Loss of Provisions (9:1-2)

One of the first indicators that God is withdrawing is that they begin to lose their provisions. Maybe Hosea is speaking at the time of harvest, and people are celebrating in anticipation of what they expect to bring in. It's possible that the crops look especially good. However, God, through Hosea, basically says, "Stop celebrating." *Rejoice not, O Israel.*

It is not shocking for the nations (the Gentile world) to celebrate a harvest by giving credit to fertility gods instead of to the true God. This is sinful, and they will be accountable for this. But the people of God, to whom He has made Himself known, will bear a heavy penalty for such brazen disregard and disobedience. God reminds them that they are not like the other peoples. They have a special responsibility due to their unique favored and covenantal relationship with Him.

Amos 3:2 *"You only have I known of all the families of the earth; therefore I will punish you for all your iniquities."*

We also, as the people of God, have special responsibilities. This isn't just an Old Testament message. Jesus said, *Everyone to whom much was given, of him much will be required* (Luke 12:48). It's also seen in the book of Hebrews.

Hebrews 12:6 *For the Lord disciplines the one he loves, and chastises every son whom he receives.*

If you live in sin and don't experience the discipline of God, you are giving evidence that you are illegitimate, and don't belong to the Lord at all.

Recognize the Reason for the Loss

Israel is suffering because they have played the harlot. They have gone after the Baals, thinking that assimilation into the surrounding culture would lead to prosperity. He takes away provision in order to wake them up to the true source of their bounty. God's discipline in the life of the nation is meant to lead to repentance, to awaken them to the fact that He is the true God, the only God, and the One who has supplied for them all along.

Hosea 4:12 (NAS) *My people consult their wooden idol, and their diviner's wand informs them; For a spirit of harlotry has led them astray, and they have played the harlot, departing from their God.*

Hosea 2:9 *Therefore, I will take back my grain in its time, and my wine in its season, and I will take away my wool and my flax, which were to cover her nakedness.*

The Loss of Their Place (9:3)

Not only are they going to lose provision, they're going to lose their place, their land—*the land of the LORD*. The Lord could not communicate their future in a more straightforward way. Egypt symbolizes captivity. The reference to Assyria tells them that God will do this through the Assyrians.

The Loss of the Possibility of Legitimate Worship (9:4-5)

Yet, just as God abandons a people by withdrawing material provision and blessing when they have no regard for God, so God abandons a people by withdrawing spiritual provision and blessing when they have no regard for it.

Israel has had the freedom to worship in the way God prescribed, but they have failed to do it. Because of their sin and disobedience, that privilege will be taken away. They will lose the possibility of going to the temple to engage in the various festivals and the times of worship that God ordained. *Drink offerings*—gone (9:4). *Sacrifices*—gone (9:4). *First fruits offerings* of bread—gone (9:4). *Festivals*—gone (9:5). *Feasts*—gone (9:5). While in captivity, they will lose the privilege of the possibility of legitimate worship.

Has your nation been graced with freedoms from God? If so, the church needs to ask itself what it is doing with these privileges and opportunities to serve God without restriction.

The Loss of Their Imaginary Security (9:6-7)

Like much of the 9th chapter, this verse is difficult to translate. Perhaps what Hosea has in mind is the thoughts of the people. They have been paying tribute and making agreements with Egypt and Assyria, imagining that they are moving away from destruction. Despite the messages from God through Hosea, Israel believes it can escape. But God again says figuratively that they will go into captivity (Egypt) and be buried (*Memphis* is an ancient Egyptian capital famous as a burial place). The riches they have trusted in (the *silver* they have piled up, their *tents*) will be left behind, overrun with prickly weeds, with *thorns* in their tents. They have valued the things that they count precious instead of God, and God is saying in effect, "What will your treasure do for you when you are taken out of your land?"

We remember (Romans 8:31) that *If God is for us, who can be against us?* But if God is against you, who can be for you? Who can save you? Not your silver, not your housing, not your alliances with Assyria and Egypt. In fact, they are just instruments of the Lord to bring about His discipline.

WHAT CLEARLY INDICATES THAT GOD IS DEPARTING (9:7-9)

Verse 7 tells us that there is certainty to all of this. *The days of punishment have come.* It's arrived, and *Israel shall know it.* There's a clear indicator that God is withdrawing. It is this: Their response to His Word.

Insults for the man of God

Diminishing sensitivity to God and to His Word is one of the signs of God's withdrawal in the life of a nation and that the end has come. God gives them over to their own stubbornness. They don't want the Word of God, and He will remove it from them.

In verse 7, some think Hosea means that Israel has a multiplication of false prophets who are madmen and fools. While they should be watching for the nation, instead, their ways represent a fowler's snare. That's one way to read this.

There is a second way to understand these verses. This man is described in verse 8 as a watchman of Ephraim with God, and in verse 7 as a man of the spirit. So, it's better to see this as a glimpse into what Hosea himself has experienced in terms of Israel's view of him. As Hosea and the other prophets preach to them, they function as true watchmen with God for the northern kingdom. While they do God's bidding, people respond with insults. Israel's sin has set them at odds with the Lord's prophets to such a degree that they hate the prophets.

For example, notice what we read when Elijah was sent by God to confront Ahab.

1 Kings 18:17 *When Ahab saw Elijah, Ahab said to him, "Is it you, you troubler of Israel?*

¹⁸ *And he answered, "I have not troubled Israel, but you have, and your father's house, because you have abandoned the commandments of the Lord and followed the Baals."*

This is not an isolated incident. I Kings 22 relates the story of King Ahab of Israel and King Jehoshaphat of Judah, and their joint venture in war toward Aram. Jehoshaphat asks that they inquire of the Lord. King Ahab said, *"There is yet one man by whom we may inquire of the LORD, Micaiah the son of Imlah, but I hate him, for he never prophesies good concerning me, but evil"* (1 Kings 22:8).

Viewing men of God as fools is one of the signs that God is judging a people. Where people give in to sin, this is their view of the ministry of the Word of God. They think that it's madness and foolishness. They hate it. When someone continues to choose sin, they begin to despise the one who would speak the truth. One of the true indicators of your spiritual condition is who you love or don't love to be around. Do you seek the counsel of someone who'll tell you what the Scriptures say, or what you want to hear?

Intrigue toward the man of God (9:8)

They didn't just hate Hosea. They were lying in wait for him. It's as if a *fowler's snare* has been set on all his paths because there's *hatred in the house of*

103

his God. The *house* refers to the land of Israel itself. A nation being abandoned by God, so hates men of God, that they will destroy them if given the opportunity. If you read the Book of Jeremiah, you'll see this is what happens in a sinful nation when a man speaks the truth of God's Word.

This behavior is seen not only in the Old Testament. It will always be true in human experience. In 2 Timothy 4:9-15, Paul writes to Timothy warning him to beware of Alexander the coppersmith. He did much harm to Paul and strongly opposed his message.

Hebrews 11:36 *Others suffered mocking and flogging, and even chains and imprisonment.* [37] *They were stoned, they were sawn in two, they were killed with the sword. They went about in skins of sheep and goats, destitute, afflicted, mistreated—* [38] *of whom the world was not worthy—wandering about in deserts and mountains, and in dens and caves of the earth.*

Luke 9:5 *And wherever they do not receive you, when you leave that town shake off the dust from your feet as a testimony against them."*

This happens to a land even to this day. When the Word of God is declared and a people reject it, spurn it, abuse and afflict those who deliver it, God judges by removing it.

Amos 8:11 *"Behold, the days are coming," declares the Lord GOD, "when I will send a famine on the land—not a famine of bread, nor a thirst for water, but of hearing the words of the LORD."*

God's Word is a blessing. You see, when the word of God is still present, there is at least hope. Perhaps if someone will listen, there can be repentance. The word of God is powerful.

Iniquity that calls for punishment (9:9)

This verse has yet another description of their iniquity. *As in the days of Gibeah* refers to an incident in Judges 19-20. Someone had shown hospitality to a Levite and his concubine (slave wife). The bisexuals in Gibeah surrounded the house and demanded to have relations with him. He sent out his concubine, and they raped and murdered her. After he found her on the doorstep the next morning, he loaded the body onto his animal and took it with him. When he reached where he was headed, he cut up her body and sent the pieces out to the various tribes of the nation, calling for judgment on the Gibeonites.

Judges 19:30 *And all who saw it said, "Such a thing has never happened or been seen from the day that the people of Israel came up out of the land of Egypt until this day; consider it, take counsel, and speak."*

God compares Israel's corrupt behavior to that of the Gibeonites.

Where the Word of God is, there is hope. If you truly are a child of God and don't renounce sin, God will discipline you. He will train you. You'll be a student in His school of grace.

Titus 2:11-14 *"For the grace of God has appeared, bringing salvation for all people, training us to renounce ungodliness and worldly passions, and to live self-controlled, upright, and godly lives in the present age, waiting for our blessed hope, the appearing of the glory of our great God and Savior Jesus Christ, who gave himself for us to redeem us from all lawlessness and to purify for himself a people for his own possession who are zealous for good works."*

Has He been striving with you? If so, will you listen, or do you want Him to leave you alone? Exposure to God's Word is His grace to you. It means there is hope.

14

When God Takes Your Glory Away

(9:10-17)

Sinful man is notoriously forgetful, and he is notoriously guilty of misplaced credit. How often, in our moment of need, we have said, "I'll never forget this lesson. I see clearly now where I've gone astray. I know, Lord, that from this point forward, my life must be completely subjected to You in this area." But after our circumstances have changed, we soon forget. And what we clearly see as the blessing of God in the beginning of something, we often attribute to ourselves over time, saying, "Look what I've done." We are notoriously forgetful and notoriously guilty of misplaced credit, crediting ourselves with what only God can do.

This is so characteristic of man that God warns about it repeatedly. He warned the people of Israel about it at the very beginning, before they entered the Promised Land.

Deuteronomy 8:11 *"Take care lest you forget the LORD your God by not keeping his commandments and his rules and his statutes, which I command you today, 12 lest, when you have eaten and are full and have built good houses and live in them, 13 and when your herds and flocks multiply and your silver and gold is multiplied and all that you have is multiplied, 14 then your heart be lifted up, and you forget the LORD your God, who brought you out of the land of Egypt, out of the house of slavery, 15 who led you through the great and terrifying wilderness, with its fiery serpents and scorpions and thirsty ground where there was no water, who brought you water out of the flinty rock, 16 who fed you in the wilderness with manna that your fathers did not know, that he might humble you and test you, to do you good in the end. 17 Beware lest you say in your heart, 'My power and the might of my hand have gotten me this wealth.' 18 You shall remember the LORD your God, for it is he who gives you power to get wealth, that he* *may confirm his covenant that he swore to your fathers, as it is this day.* [19] *And if you forget the LORD your God and go after other gods and serve them and worship them, I solemnly warn you today that you shall surely perish.* [20] *Like the nations that the LORD makes to perish before you, so shall you perish, because you would not obey the voice of the LORD your God."*

What we forget is that only God has inherent glory. Any real glory we possess is glory that God gives. It is an expression of the goodness and grace of God, and it is not sustained apart from the sheer goodness and grace of God.

Every beauty, every virtue, every strength, every benefit, every advantage, anything desirable, has been given to an individual, or to a people. If we forget this, one of the ways God judges is by taking away that glory. Israel will soon learn this lesson the hard way, as God causes the glory He gave her to depart. God declares His judgment upon the northern kingdom by declaring that her glory will *fly away*. (9:11)

THE BEGINNINGS OF RUINED PROMISE (9:10)

Once again God gives a sad history lesson about the ways of this people.

Good Beginnings

In the beginning, Israel represented promise.

> ***Like Grapes in the Wilderness***—In the wilderness, grapes are a delight, an unexpected pleasure.
> ***Like the First Fruit on a New Fig Tree***—There is delight— pleasure. There is a positive and hopeful beginning. There is a sense of blessing. There is fruit. The Lord says, *I saw your fathers* like that.

Detestable Behavior

That sense of promise was ruined by detestable behavior, the detestable behavior that God is addressing through Hosea.

The Lord reminds them of their past: at Baal-peor they entered into idolatry and into relationships with foreign women. He brings up their past infidelity because it's still with them. The people have not changed. Hosea is addressing the very same issue: idolatry, sexual immorality, and all kinds of spiritual and moral unfaithfulness. We read about Baal-peor in Numbers 25.

Numbers 25:1 *While Israel lived in Shittim, the people began to whore with the daughters of Moab. ² These invited the people to the sacrifices of their gods, and the people ate and bowed down to their gods. ³ So Israel yoked himself to Baal of Peor. And the anger of the LORD was kindled against Israel. ⁴ And the LORD said to Moses, "Take all the chiefs of the people and hang them in the sun before the LORD, that the fierce anger of the LORD may turn away from Israel." ⁵ And Moses said to the judges of Israel, "Each of you kill those of his men who have yoked themselves to Baal of Peor." ⁶ And behold, one of the people of Israel came and brought a Midianite woman to his family, in the sight of Moses and in the sight of the whole congregation of the people of Israel, while they were weeping in the entrance of the tent of meeting. ⁷ When Phinehas the son of Eleazar, son of Aaron the priest, saw it, he rose and left the congregation and took a spear in his hand ⁸ and went after the man of Israel into the chamber and pierced both of them, the man of Israel and the woman through her belly. Thus the plague on the people of Israel was stopped. ⁹ Nevertheless, those who died by the plague were twenty-four thousand.*

This was a strategic temptation, birthed from the wicked prophet Balaam, an enemy of the people of God.

Numbers 31:14 *And Moses was angry with the officers of the army, the commanders of thousands and the commanders of hundreds, who had come from service in the war. ¹⁵ Moses said to them, "Have you let all the women live? ¹⁶ Behold, these, <u>on Balaam's advice</u>, caused the people of Israel to act treacherously against the LORD in the incident of Peor, and so the plague came among the congregation of the LORD.*

And while we note what this kind of sin produced in the life of the northern kingdom, we dare not ignore the fact that it is a warning to our own lives. Paul used this very incident to warn the Corinthians concerning idolatry and immorality.

1 Corinthians 10:1 *For I want you to know, brothers, that our fathers were all under the cloud, and all passed through the sea, ² and all were baptized into Moses in the cloud and in the sea, ³ and all ate the same spiritual food, ⁴ and all drank the same spiritual drink. For they drank from the spiritual Rock that followed them, and the Rock was Christ. ⁵ Nevertheless, with most of them God was not pleased, for they were overthrown in the wilderness. ⁶ Now these things took place as examples for us, that we might not desire evil as they did. ⁷ Do not be idolaters as some of them were; as it is written, "The people sat down to eat and drink and rose up to play." ⁸ We must not indulge in sexual immorality as some of them did, and twenty-three thousand fell in a single day. ⁹ We* *must not put Christ to the test, as some of them did and were destroyed by serpents, [10] nor grumble, as some of them did and were destroyed by the Destroyer. [11] Now these things happened to them as an example, but they were written down for our instruction, on whom the end of the ages has come. [12] Therefore let anyone who thinks that he stands take heed lest he fall. [13] No temptation has overtaken you that is not common to man. God is faithful, and he will not let you be tempted beyond your ability, but with the temptation he will also provide the way of escape, that you may be able to endure it. [14] Therefore, my beloved, flee from idolatry.*

Christ warned the church at Pergamum from this very incident.

Revelation 2:14 *But I have a few things against you: you have some there who hold the teaching of Balaam, who taught Balak to put a stumbling block before the sons of Israel, so that they might eat food sacrificed to idols and practice sexual immorality. [15] So also you have some who hold the teaching of the Nicolaitans. [16] Therefore repent. If not, I will come to you soon and war against them with the sword of my mouth.*

They loved what was detestable, and *they became detestable like the thing they loved.* A detestable person is one characterized by what God hates. How does someone become a detestable person? By loving and desiring and devoting themselves to what is detestable. It is true both to say that detestable people desire detestable things, and that we become conformed more and more to that which we set our hearts on.

What kind of a person are you, and what kind of a person are you becoming? We have all seen it: young men and young women who once had joy in their eyes, and a measure of innocence in their conscience, and therefore on their countenance. But suddenly there's a hardening. They look older than they are and wear sin on their countenance because they have bought the lie that there is lasting satisfaction outside of obedience to Christ, and they are running after things God hates.

It would be wonderful if this were the story of just one generation that forgot the Lord in the land of plenty. It would be wonderful if only one generation believed the lies regarding other gods and traded the glory of the incorruptible God for worthless things. But it isn't just one generation. This is what characterizes every generation of men. It characterizes every unbeliever, and even believers can fall prey to it.

THE CONTINUATION OF RUINED PROMISE (9:11-13)

So, what does God do to get Israel's attention?

Departing Glory (9:11)

Israel has imagined that their glory is their own! They think all the blessings they have enjoyed, all of the favor and all the advantages, are theirs by right or are given by the Baals. Israel doesn't stop to understand that these are gifts from the Lord, gifts that they do not deserve. Now, because of their sin, and especially because of their stubbornness and refusal to repent, God will take that glory away. He had also said this earlier in the book.

Hosea 4:6 *My people are destroyed for lack of knowledge; because you have rejected knowledge, I reject you from being a priest to me. And since you have forgotten the law of your God, I also will forget your children. ⁷ The more they increased, the more they sinned against me; I will change their glory into shame.*

Devastated Future (9:11-12)

It's interesting that when God talks about departing from them, about their glory flying away from them, it is in the immediate context of the devastation of future generations. Sin's devastating effects are felt by the children when God judges a culture. The Lord said there will be *no birth, no pregnancy, no conception*; that even if they bring up children, he will *bereave them till none is left*. The future of any culture is the next generation. Our children are our glory, gift, treasure, and wealth, but people often don't realize that. What can a nation expect, except judgment, when they

- Murder their own children or treat them as if they are no treasure at all
- Wait until they are in their 30's or 40's to have children, and then have only one or two, because they think having children is something to do only for their own pleasure
- Indoctrinate children in wickedness instead of in God's Word
- Take care of themselves while their children suffer
- Sacrifice their children on the altars of their own pleasures

Wasted Privilege (9:13)

Ephraim *was like a young palm planted in a meadow*. What a beautiful thought—a young palm planted in a beautiful place. The Lord gave them the choice spot. Any kind of trade between Egypt and places to the north requires travel through their land. Even today, it's amazing how much of what's in the news relates to this one small place. Why? Because the Lord gave them the choice spot. Yet they have wasted it.

This is not the first place in scripture where we see this. Read Deuteronomy 32:1-18, and especially note verse 8.

Deuteronomy 32:8 *When the Most High gave to the nations their inheritance, when he divided mankind, he fixed the borders of the peoples according to the number of the sons of God.*

That is, He arranged everything with Israel in mind. Yet, as verses 15 and 18 of that chapter says, *Jeshurun* [that is, Israel] *grew fat, and kicked ... then he forsook God who made him and scoffed at the Rock of his salvation. You were unmindful of the Rock that bore you, and you forgot the God who gave you birth.*

THE CONCLUSION OF RUINED PROMISE (9:14-17)

Hosea prays, *Give them, O Lord—What will you give?* It's a prayer that's cut off. He begins, but he doesn't know what to ask for. It is, in fact, a prayer that calls for judgment. It's like the imprecatory psalms where the psalmist is calling for God to bring justice. Hosea is full of emotion over what he's seeing, and the only thing he can pray for is for God to discipline His people. What does a people become when they rebel against God in a determined way?

Hateful to godly people (9:14)

Hosea is a godly prophet. He detests what he's seeing in the life of his people. So then he asks for this: *Give them a miscarrying womb and dry breasts.* As we go after detestable things, one result is that we become hateful to godly people. Our life represents what godly people detest.

Hateful to holy God (9:15)

Notice in verse 15 that it's the Lord speaking. *...There I began to hate them. Because of the wickedness of their deeds I will drive them out of my house; all their princes are rebels.* They are living in a way that is hateful to godly people; living in a way that's hateful to God Himself.

Holding to a dark future (9:16)

For God to love you is to choose you. For God to not love you is to not choose you. That means they have a dark future. When you refuse to hear the Lord, and you hold onto your sin, you are holding on to your own destruction.

They will be like a tree whose *root is dried up*, with the result that it will *bear no fruit*. Some of the few *children* that they have will die.

Having nothing in the end (9:17)

In this verse, we're back to Hosea speaking. *My God will reject them*. They will be *wanderers among the nations*. They will lose their land, lose its fruit, lose all the blessings and all the privileges. They will be dispersed among the nations.

When you refuse to listen to God who gave you everything, when you won't repent, as you seek to hold onto what you think you've done for yourself, you end up with nothing. Don't forget Him. Your glory is not inherent. Don't attribute to yourself what only God could have done. Maybe you were willing to listen to Him in your crisis, but now you think you have it under control. But the reason why you were where you were is because you thought you had it under control. Israel in this chapter is in trouble, verse 17, *because they have not listened to him*. Humble yourself before God and listen to Him. Are you pursuing detestable things and becoming a detestable person? Pursue the Lord Jesus Christ, and as you do, you'll be conformed to his beautiful image.

15
Judged by Prosperity
(10:1-10)

God deals with people who don't know it, in ways that they don't recognize to be Him. This includes testing them in more than one way.

Some people show promise of being fruitful. They seem teachable in hard times but prove fruitless when easier times come. As in the parable of the sower, the cares of this life, like weeds, choke them, so they bear no fruit.

It is a story repeated again and again in human history and on the pages of Scripture. And it's a story that we find in chapter 10 of Hosea. The people of Israel have been tested without knowing it. They have been tested by material prosperity and have proven unfaithful. God has allowed them to be blessed, but they have been practicing idolatry. God was taking note, and He now testifies against them based upon what they have done with His blessings.

THE FRUITLESSNESS OF ISRAEL (10:1-2)

God's Gracious Faithfulness (10:1a)

Once again, Hosea describes the nation in terms of a promising beginning—the potential for fruitfulness. God granted them favor, His protection, and His special provision. He granted them a choice spot in the world, perfectly fit for the nation's prosperity. Because God, in His grace, has set them up for blessing and has provided for them and protected them, they have blossomed materially. They are a *luxuriant vine that yields its fruit.*

Israel's Sinful Unfaithfulness (10:1b-2)

The nation Hosea is speaking to is just coming out of extremely prosperous times, and they no doubt think that it is a commentary on their current status before God and on the promise of future blessing. But the Lord knows what they have done with the peace and the prosperity that He granted them. Israel has multiplied its sinning by taking God's blessings and allowing those very blessings to estrange their hearts from God. They have built *altars* and *pillars* that pay tribute to gods that are no gods, spending God's blessings on idolatry instead of on the pure worship He demands and deserves. Their worship is mixed—going after the Baals but doing so in the name of the true God. God completely rejects this mixture.

God's blessing has only proven their idolatrous heart. *Their heart is false* (10:2). The word for false (חָלַק ḥā·laq) can mean slippery, smooth. Their heart is deceptive. They say they know and love the Lord and are pursuing Him, but their heart is false. Their spiritual immorality, sexual immorality, and moral pursuit of that which is detestable to God, all demonstrate that as verse 4 says, *They utter mere words*.

We see this every day. People are granted prosperity, but it doesn't turn out for their spiritual good. They take what God gives them and then substitute those blessings for God. Their lives show this. Maybe a man asks God for a good job, and He grants it. But now the job comes first, not the Lord, and the man abandons the church. Or maybe a family uses increased income to purchase things that take them away from spiritual faithfulness. They are now gone to their weekend place or out on their boat, substituting their pleasures for God. Or maybe they are blessed with a loving family but substitute it for God. They spend all their time celebrating their family instead of seeing their everlasting place in God's family as having the priority. Christ must be preeminent in everything.

Israel does not recognize it, but as they are being fruitful (10:1), the Lord has been examining them the entire time, and their guilt has been established. Their *heart* (10:2) has proven to be *false*. Their pleasures, their prosperity, and their idols are their gods. As a result, they now bear their guilt.

Perhaps you are being tested right now, not by adversity, but by a sudden prosperity.

Proverbs 27:21 *The crucible is for silver, and the furnace is for gold, and a man is tested by his praise.*

Proverbs 30:7 *Two things I ask of you; deny them not to me before I die:* [8] *Remove far from me falsehood and lying; give me neither poverty nor riches; feed me with the food that is needful for me,* [9] *lest I be full and deny you and say, "Who is the LORD?" or lest I be poor and steal and profane the name of my God.*

Israel's True Heart Condition (10:2)

Why don't people do well with prosperity? It is because of a false heart. Israel's heart was on trial. So is ours, daily.

Matthew 6:19 *"Do not lay up for yourselves treasures on earth, where moth and rust destroy and where thieves break in and steal,* [20] *but lay up for yourselves treasures in heaven, where neither moth nor rust destroys and where thieves do not break in and steal.* [21] *For where your treasure is, there your heart will be also."*

To know where your heart is, look at what you treasure most. It is easy to say that the Lord is your treasure when you have no possibility of any other kind of treasure. But when God blesses you and puts some other kind of treasure right in your path, we will find out what you really value; <u>whether your heart is true or false.</u>

People are notorious for being liars about their treasure. Because their heart tells lies, God says their heart is false. We have seen people put a positive spin on their wrong priorities. Are you doing that?

God says Israel's response to prosperity has established their guilt, so He will *break down their altars and destroy their pillars* (10:2). He will take away what they have treasured and substituted for Him.

THE FUTURE OF ISRAEL (10:3-10)

Having noted Israel's fruitlessness and unfaithfulness, He now tells specifically what their future will be. What does God do with His people when they misunderstand and misuse His blessings, when they substitute what He gives them for God Himself, when they are unfaithful in their times of prosperity?

They will be forced to acknowledge an empty trust in wicked leaders (10:3-4).

They will say, "We have no king, for we do not fear the Lord; and a king—what could he do for us?" They utter mere words; with empty oaths they make covenants; so

115

judgment springs up like poisonous weeds in the furrows of the field. God will work in such a way that they will be forced to acknowledge that they have placed an empty trust in wicked leaders. Verse 4 is difficult, because we are not sure whether he is saying that the kings are no help because their words are empty (they break covenants), or whether he is saying the people will acknowledge this about their own behavior. The latter would tie back to the idea in the previous verse that *we do not fear the Lord.*

Either way, it's clear that this is a people characterized by not keeping their commitments because they do not fear God. As a result, *judgment springs up like poisonous weeds in the furrows of the field.* Wicked people don't understand the fear of the Lord, so they break their commitments, and as a result they are judged. They will be forced to acknowledge all of this.

They will be forced to acknowledge an empty trust in wicked idols (10:5-6)

10:5 *The inhabitants of Samaria tremble for the calf of Beth-aven. Its people mourn for it, and so do its idolatrous priests—those who rejoiced over it and over its glory—for it has departed from them.*

Beth-aven is another word for Bethel. The place Jacob named Bethel (House of God) has become Beth-aven (House of Vanity). The word for *idolatrous priests* is used only for priests of Baal. These spiritual leaders who have promoted the worship of Baal—*those who rejoiced over it and over its glory*—will be mourning, because *it has departed from them* (10:5). *The thing itself*—the calf— *shall be carried to Assyria as tribute to the great king*—the king of Assyria. *Ephraim shall be put to shame, and Israel shall be ashamed of his idol* (10:6). They have worshiped this calf at Bethel, but soon the calf won't be there to worship. The conquering Assyrians will carry it away along with the other idols of peoples they've conquered. It will belong to the king of Assyria, as tribute to him. The people of Israel will be put to shame for every bit of trust they ever placed in their false religion.

The end of verse 6, which says *Israel shall be ashamed of his idol,* could also be translated, *Israel shall be ashamed of his counsel.* That is, they will come to see that the agreements they are trying to make with Assyria and with Egypt, misplace their trust. They have trusted in men and in false gods instead of in the living God.

They will witness the destruction of both vices (10:7-8)

They have trusted in wicked leaders and in wicked idols. Those two things are brought together in the picture of destruction in verses 7 and 8. *Samaria's king* (the king of the northern kingdom) *shall perish like a twig on the face of the waters*. He will be as helpless as a twig that a child tosses into a stream and watches as it dances around and heads downstream. He will be swept away.

Along with this removal of the leadership will be a removal of all the idolatrous places that the Lord has hated. *The high places of Aven, the sin of Israel, shall be destroyed*. These high places will be overgrown with *thorn and thistle*, and they will *say to the mountains, "Cover us," and to the hills, "Fall on us."* They will face fearful judgment as their high places are destroyed by God. This is ironic, because the destruction of those high places is a job that was given to Israel.

Deuteronomy 12:1 *"These are the statutes and rules that you shall be careful to do in the land that the LORD, the God of your fathers, has given you to possess, all the days that you live on the earth. ² You shall surely destroy all the places where the nations whom you shall dispossess served their gods, on the high mountains and on the hills and under every green tree. ³ You shall tear down their altars and dash in pieces their pillars and burn their Asherim with fire. You shall chop down the carved images of their gods and destroy their name out of that place. ⁴ You shall not worship the LORD your God in that way."*

There's not to be this mixture of the worship of the true God and the worship of the nations.

They will feel God's discipline because they haven't changed (10:9-10)

From the days of Gibeah, you have sinned, O Israel. At Gibeah there was the brutal rape and murder of the Levite's concubine (Judges 19-20). God traces their sinful behavior back to such an event, and *they have continued*. What was true of them at Gibeah is still true. There is *double iniquity*. The best explanation for *double iniquity* is that they are still guilty of their initial sin at Gibeah (because they never really repented), and they are also guilty of their current sin.

As a result, *Shall not the war against the unjust*—or the children of injustice—*overtake them in Gibeah?* The Lord has dealt with them and warned them, but they won't turn. So, isn't it right that they be judged?

In 10:10, the Lord says, *When I please, I will discipline them.* The only thing standing between hardhearted, willful sinning and devastating judgment is the patience of God. That's all. When He's ready, discipline will come.

At times, sinners actually say to themselves—both in the Old Testament and in the New Testament, and also today— "Where is the judgment of God?" Famous atheist Robert G. Ingersoll was a traveling lecturer. One of the things he loved to do was to dare God to strike him dead in the next five minutes. He would hold up his watch and at the end of five minutes he would set it down as if he had some triumph and say, "Where is God?" To that, Dr. Joseph Parker answered, "Did the gentleman think he could exhaust the patience of the eternal God in five minutes?"[14]

No, just because you haven't felt God's heavy hand yet, doesn't mean that you won't if you continue in your sin. When the Lord pleases, without any advance notice, you may fiercely and finally feel what your sins deserve.

God is the One disciplining, and He tells them how. *Nations shall be gathered against them….* What's happening on the world scene, with the movement of the nations, is not happening on its own. God is directing the affairs of this world.

If you continue in your sin, just realize all that is at God's disposal to bring His discipline upon you. He's the one who gives you power to get wealth, and when we turn a deaf ear to God, He is able to discipline His people.

Nations shall be gathered against them when they are bound up for their double iniquity. Iniquity was their path generations ago, and it's still their character. For this double iniquity, they will be bound up. The picture is of being yoked to something. They will be *bound* to their sin for the purpose of discipline and judgment. Verse 11, which we'll look at in the next lesson, continues the image of being bound or yoked. The Lord will yoke them to their double iniquity. He will punish them.

APPLYING IT

We're all being tested every day. God tests His people in order to prove us, to demonstrate what He's done in our lives. Satan brings temptation. He

---

[14] This story appears in various places, with the time allotted varying. One source is John Phillips, Exploring Psalms: An Expository Commentary, vol. 2 (Kregel Publications, reprinted 2011), p. 233.

would have us stumble and fall. We're being tested, not just by difficult things, but when the wind is at our back. We're tested when the obstacles have been removed, when there are unexpected blessings, and when we are prosperous.

When God gives you more, do you prove more faithful, or do you begin to serve those things instead of serving Him? Our God is jealous for us. In His own time, God will discipline us by taking away anything we substitute for Him.

In our lives, Christ is to be preeminent in everything. That means in every area of your life, it's Jesus first. This means Jesus first in your marriage, in the raising of your children, in your job, in your education, in your friendships, and in what you own and possess. In fact, in a sense, not just first. He's all there is. May we be able to say with an honest heart, "Lord, I value nothing more than I value You. You are my treasure. I serve You."

16
Sowing and Reaping
(10:11-15)

God is communicating in the clearest way possible using straightforward language and illustrations from the people's everyday life. Theirs is an agrarian culture, and He speaks to them based upon their daily work of farming, gathering and threshing. Though we may not be as familiar with the comparisons, in God's perfect wisdom they accurately convey the message. It is simple but powerful, one that we see proven around us daily. You will reap what you sow. What you put out is what you get back.

God is calling upon those who are sowing iniquity—and He is calling to us, if we are sowing sin—to repent, to change course, and to walk in a new way. This is not just a call to a new attitude. It's a call to a change of mind and heart that results in changed actions. Repentance is not hidden. Where there's a new man or a new woman, there is a new way of living.

We know from God's Word that repentance ultimately is something granted by God, a work of His grace. Yet Scripture sets repentance before us again and again as a choice. Every day is a choice between life and death. The way of the Lord is the way of life, and the way of disobedience is the way of death. Almighty God, who needs nothing, so cares for His creatures and so cares for His children, that He cries out to us, calling upon us to choose life. Which way will you choose?

Deuteronomy 30:19 *I call heaven and earth to witness against you today, that I have set before you life and death, blessing and curse. Therefore choose life, that you and your offspring may live, 20 loving the LORD your God, obeying his voice and holding fast to* *him, for he is your life and length of days, that you may dwell in the land that the* LORD *swore to your fathers, to Abraham, to Isaac, and to Jacob, to give them."*

God says to His people Israel, *choose life*. That means to choose God. What does it mean to *choose life* today? It means to choose the Lord. Listen to Him. Follow Him. Cling to Him, for He is your life. He is the *length* of our *days*.

TO CHOOSE SIN IS TO CHOOSE THE HARD WAY (10:11)

The Lord again goes back to His beginning days with the nation, better days, days when they were responsive to Him. In those days, *Ephraim was a trained calf*, a teachable calf that was almost a pet. This contrasts with Jeremiah 31:18, where Ephraim was *like an untrained calf*. Here in Hosea 10, He is reflecting on the time when Israel was responsive and He *spared her fair neck*. He has been abundantly good to them, abundantly patient with them, but they are forfeiting this through sin.

The Way of Obedience Is the Way of Positive Responsibility

Although they were given a choice spot, designed specifically for them by God, they were not without responsibility. The responsibilities pictured are positive. It's much easier for an animal to *thresh* than to *plow* or to *harrow*. The animal must spin a wheel or walk over grain on a hard surface (a threshing floor) to separate the grain from the stalks and chaff. There is food available (the Law specifies that the animal must not be muzzled), there's a smaller area to walk, and there's no heavy work involved. It is work, but easier work. As it is pictured here, it is something the animal loves to do.

That is the way of an obedient and faithful life with the Lord. It is not a life without responsibilities, but it is a way of joyful and fulfilling responsibility. This picture is one of God assigning the easier work on purpose. He spared the neck of the animal from the yoke.

Remember that when Adam and Eve were first formed, they were given responsibility by God. In a paradise, they had work to do. Their work was fulfilling and joyful to them.

Genesis 2:15 *The* LORD *God took the man and put him in the garden of Eden to work it and keep it.* ¹⁶ *And the* LORD *God commanded the man, saying, "You may surely eat of every tree of the garden,* ¹⁷ *but of the tree of the knowledge of good and evil you shall not eat, for in the day that you eat of it you shall surely die."* ¹⁸ *Then the*

LORD *God said, "It is not good that the man should be alone; I will make him a helper fit for him."*

The Way of Sin Is the Way of Negative Responsibility

Because of the ungrateful, stubborn and sinful ways of the people, God will now spare them no longer. They are going to be yoked to the life they have chosen. They will now have to *plow* and *harrow*. To harrow is for the animal to pull a tool like a big rake that breaks up and smooths the soil. This is much harder than threshing, and not a task that the animal would prefer. It is a simple but powerful picture, one that like the rest of the Word of God, is completely accurate and truthful. God is saying that to choose your sin is to choose a way that is foolish. His ways are pleasant and fulfilling, joyfully productive. But the way of sin is painful, difficult, and empty. When you choose the hard way of sin, at the end of it there's no blessing. There's nothing productive nor joyful that will fulfill the human heart.

Israel is choosing sin and now will plow. Many people today could testify that they have chosen the way of sin and have found it to be a very hard way.

TO CHOOSE REPENTANCE IS TO CHOOSE A BLESSED WAY (10:12)

Amazingly, even now, as Hosea announces this difficult way, God wants a different outcome for His people. He would delight to bless them, giving them a way that is fulfilling and joyful, one that they do not deserve. Maybe you have been on that course of sin. It's already been hard for you and unfulfilling, but you're still believing sin's lie, and you remain on this course that at its end will prove you a fool. But God offers the way to a better outcome.

God points them to repentance as the way to have better days. It is the way of submission, faithfulness and obedience. This is not behaviorism nor moralism. It's a new way of faith. It's believing God, listening to God, loving God, following God. And God is telling them that they can be sure that they will reap what they sow. If they sow righteousness, then they'll reap the experience of God's faithful love. God is ready to bless their land with righteousness like rain, but this requires action on the part of the people.

- They must *break up the fallow ground.* The ground of their hearts has been hardened toward God. They must soften their hearts.

- They must *sow righteousness*. God promises blessing for obedience. God not only calls us to what's right because it is right, but also blesses as we do it. Faithfulness to Him brings goodness that is multiplied, abundant, undeserved and merciful. To *sow righteousness* is to turn from your sin to do the things that please the Lord—and we know what pleases Him, because He's told us in His Word.

- Israel needs to *seek the Lord* immediately, and He will *come and rain righteousness* down upon them, showing Himself present and mighty. Repentance is not mere legalistic moralism nor behaviorism. Repentance is a new way because you are walking after Him. It's the path of believing God, listening to God, loving God and following God.

This process is not instant. It takes time to plow and sow. This is a determined, long-term view of life, but it yields great bounty. When you serve the Lord, there is never an empty return. It's not a promise that you'll be healthy and wealthy, the most successful person in your business with everything always going the way you want. No, He promises you Himself, that He will *come.* You *seek* Him, turning to Him that He may *rain righteousness upon you,* filling your life with His own character. You will find that all His promises are true. Do you need to hear this? Will you listen?

TO CHOOSE STUBBORNNESS IS TO CHOOSE A TERRIBLE END (10:13-15)

These verses may not seem like a gracious word, but they are. As God, through Hosea, sets life and death before them, He reminds Israel of why they are where they are, and where they will soon be. People don't like to hear why they are in trouble, and they don't like to hear of the trouble they are headed for. It sometimes makes us angry, but we need to hear it. There's the way of sin and the way of repentance. If you don't choose repentance, you've chosen to be stubborn, sinfully stubborn.

Where They Have Been (10:13)

Morally, the land is in a mess. Sin is bursting out everywhere as they have *plowed iniquity.* He doesn't say you've *sown* iniquity, but, "You have *plowed* iniquity." This means they've worked at it, and they have *reaped* a harvest of sin, *injustice.*

They have *eaten the fruit of lies.* They have believed lies, going after false gods, the Baals. They live like the surrounding nations who believe these fertility gods have provided all they need, even their crops. So, they've been telling lies with their lives.

Verse 13 points to the root of their problem. They've *trusted in* their *own way*, in their own military might. Israel has done this not only domestically, but in foreign affairs as they have done their best to provide security for themselves. If they had trusted in God, they would have peace and safety, but they're going to get war.

People don't like to hear why their life is in trouble, and they don't like to be faced with the crop they have sown, but they need to be. People need to see and acknowledge where they have gone astray and to be fully convinced that if they stay on the same course, the outcome is not going to be any better. Indeed, it is going to be worse.

Where They Are Headed (10:14-15)

Their <u>self-trust will lead to sure destruction (10:14)</u>. God mentions a specific earlier battle that is lost to history, one in which there were atrocities and heartless, cruel destruction of human life. The Lord set life and death before them—a choice between Himself and sin. They chose death, and they're going to get death. They will reap what they've sown. <u>Great evil will lead to great devastation (10:15).</u> They will no longer have a nation, a land or a king. They'll lose it all.

APPLYING IT

God's nature as expressed and displayed toward Israel has not changed. Just as He warned Israel, so God does with the world today. It is in upheaval and loss. It's headed toward utter destruction, the fruit of evil choices. If you choose sin, there's a lot to lose <u>in this life</u>. But if you choose sin, there is absolute, utter devastation that's <u>beyond this life</u>. It's an eternity outside of the loving, accepting presence of God. It's called hell. But God has made the way possible for us to escape all of that. Through God's sin sacrifice of His Son Jesus we can know His everlasting love. Will you listen? Will you choose life? *Sow for yourselves righteousness; reap steadfast love; break up your fallow ground, for it is time to seek the LORD, that he may come and rain righteousness upon you.*

17

The Most Overlooked Aspect of Sin
(11:1-11)

There are many overlooked aspects of sin. Man has no real idea as to the sinfulness of his sin because it blinds us to the truth. Men miss many facts about sin:

- Sin is first and foremost against God Himself. It is not an impersonal act.
- Sin is transgression, not some vague act. God has defined and identified it in His Word. Everything that violates the Word of God is sin.
- Every act of sin is worthy of death. It is not some light thing. Even the smallest act of sin has the germ of the greatest ones. It is all defiance of the Most High.
- Sin is rebellion.
- Sin is an act against the goodness and love of God, perhaps making it the most overlooked aspect and the most sinful, because it is an act of betrayal. Every act of sin is truly an act of betrayal because we are returning evil for good. It demonstrates our unfaithful nature.

As a culture we have become accustomed to betrayal, and it isn't talked about much anymore. But betrayal is hateful to God. That is what all covenant breaking is. Judas Iscariot betrayed the Lord for money, after Jesus had included him into His closest number and treated him with all of the goodness and kindness that the other eleven disciples received from Him. Demas was a betrayer when he deserted the apostle Paul, and it's what every human being is by nature.

There are numerous examples in David's Psalms. Notice Psalm 35:5-18. He prays for God's judgment against those who are pursuing him. It especially grieves David because he has loved them and prayed for them in their hard times. They're returning evil for good.

Proverbs 17:13 says: *If anyone returns evil for good, evil will not depart from his house.* God watches over that word to make sure it comes to pass.

Hosea 11 makes plain that a part of what makes Israel's sin so detestable, is that it has been done in return for all of God's goodness to them. He has been good to them. He genuinely loves Israel, yet Israel has been unfaithful to God. This truth has already been illustrated by Hosea's own marriage because his wife became a prostitute. He remains faithful and loves her, even though she has been unfaithful.

GOD'S FATHERLY GOODNESS TO ISRAEL (11:1-4)

Now God uses a different image. He is a betrayed parent, a wounded and grieved father. God compares His love for this people to that of a loving father, reminding them of His goodness. He goes back to the beginning, to the infant stages of His dealings with the nation, when He delivered them and led them out of Egypt. The Lord used this same analogy of a parent when He was delivering them.

Exodus 4:21 *And the LORD said to Moses, "When you go back to Egypt, see that you do before Pharaoh all the miracles that I have put in your power. But I will harden his heart, so that he will not let the people go. 22 Then you shall say to Pharaoh, 'Thus says the LORD, Israel is my firstborn son, 23 and I say to you, "Let my son go that he may serve me." If you refuse to let him go, behold, I will kill your firstborn son.'"*

Later, in the Book of Deuteronomy, God makes plain the reason why this father/son relationship exists between Himself and Israel. It's just because of the love of God. God loves Israel, not because they merit it, but because of His sovereign choice.

Deuteronomy 7:6 *"For you are a people holy to the LORD your God. The LORD your God has chosen you to be a people for his treasured possession, out of all the peoples who are on the face of the earth. 7 It was not because you were more in number than any other people that the LORD set his love on you and chose you, for you were the fewest of* *all peoples,* [8] *but it is because the* LORD *loves you and is keeping the oath that he swore to your fathers, that the* LORD *has brought you out with a mighty hand and redeemed you from the house of slavery, from the hand of Pharaoh king of Egypt.*

As God communicates it here, we are meant to understand that it was no cold choice, but that His heart is warm toward this people.

- God taught them to walk. He was like a father who puts down his fingers and holds that little hand so that the child learns to walk beside him. (11:3)
- God took care of them when they were not aware of it. (11:3)
  - When the people of Israel were weakened by their own sinful choices and could have been destroyed, God would strengthen them and allow them to survive.
- God dealt with them gently. (11:4) The image now changes to that of a master and an animal, as in Hosea 10:11. He's like a master who repositions the yoke in such a way that it's easier for the animal to feed.
- God fed them. (11:4) In fact, He humbled Himself (*bent down*) in order to feed them.

GOD'S FATHERLY DISCIPLINE OF ISRAEL (11:2, 5-7)

But how did Israel respond to all this goodness? With indifference and idolatry (11:2). Through the years God used prophets like Moses, and now He's using Hosea, to call out His people again and again. *The more they were called, the more they went away.* In the face of God's goodness, they have returned evil to Him. They have ignored the voice of God through His Word, being blatantly unfaithful to their Father.

This is shocking language for the God who needs nothing, who depends on no one. He is pouring out His heart like a wounded father. The true wickedness of sin is magnified because this indifference is not only against God's person or His law, but against His goodness and faithfulness. It is the height of returning evil for good.

God is going to discipline Israel with the loss of their freedom because they refused to return to Him. (11:5-7)

- They will return to captivity because they would not return to God. (11:5) They will lose both their land and their king.

- They will be consumed by the sword because they have chosen their own counsel. (11:6) Here, God uses a different analogy of feeding. In verse 4, God bent down in love and fed them, but they rejected Him. As a result of their choices, they will be fed to the ruthless sword. All their defenses will be torn down, and they will be devoured.

- They will be left to themselves because they do not truly turn to God (11:7) This is a difficult verse for translators. The ESV rendering has the people calling out to God, but He won't listen to them. Some picture it as the prophets calling out to the people, directing them to the Most High, but they don't listen to the prophets. Following the ESV, God will not listen to Israel because He knows their hearts; *they are bent on turning away from me.*

GOD'S FATHERLY COMMITMENT TO ISRAEL (11:.8-11)

The Disciplining of Israel Is Painful to God (11:8)

In verse 8 we hear God's compassionate heart. Although God will judge Israel with fearful discipline, He doesn't want to do it. He is still committed to them. It's amazing that He could love such a people.

Admah and *Zeboiim* were cities near Sodom and Gomorrah. They were destroyed when the Lord destroyed Sodom and Gomorrah. They represent complete destruction, with nothing left. The following passage tells us about it.

Deuteronomy 29:18 *Beware lest there be among you a man or woman or clan or tribe whose heart is turning away today from the LORD our God to go and serve the gods of those nations. Beware lest there be among you a root bearing poisonous and bitter fruit, *[19]* one who, when he hears the words of this sworn covenant, blesses himself in his heart, saying, 'I shall be safe, though I walk in the stubbornness of my heart.' This will lead to the sweeping away of moist and dry alike. *[20]* The LORD will not be willing to forgive him, but rather the anger of the LORD and his jealousy will smoke against that man, and the curses written in this book will settle upon him, and the LORD will blot out his name from under heaven. *[21]* And the LORD will single him out from all the tribes of Israel for calamity, in accordance with all the curses of the covenant written in this Book of the Law. *[22]* And the next generation, your children who rise up after you, and the* *foreigner who comes from a far land, will say, when they see the afflictions of that land and the sicknesses with which the LORD has made it sick— ²³ the whole land burned out with brimstone and salt, nothing sown and nothing growing, where no plant can sprout, an overthrow like that of Sodom and Gomorrah, Admah, and Zeboiim, which the LORD overthrew in his anger and wrath— ²⁴ all the nations will say, 'Why has the LORD done thus to this land? What caused the heat of this great anger?'*

His decision to judge His people, and the recoiling of His heart at the thought, seems like a conflict within God, but it is not. He is simply expressing Himself this way so we can know the fatherly heart of God toward His people.

The Disciplining of Israel Is Not the Total Destruction of Israel (11:9)

If God would give them what they deserve, and *come* to them *in wrath*, they would be utterly wiped out. But there is something within Him that counters this, and that is His *compassion* for them. It *grows warm and tender*. He won't *execute* His *burning anger*. Why? Because He is *God and not a man*. Men would not have this kind of compassion, but He is *the Holy One* in their *midst*. He says, *I will not come in wrath*. He has made promises to this people, and despite their absolute unfaithfulness, He has the power and the ability to bring all those promises to pass, and He will do it. When He does, it won't be explained by what they deserve. He is the only explanation for it.

The Disciplining of Israel Will Culminate with the Regathering of Israel (11:11)

Next, God makes two promises in verses 10 and 11. They look ahead to the time of the Millennial Kingdom when God will bring this to pass. God will come in judgment with the *roar* of a *lion*, resulting in His people turning *trembling* to Him with a fresh sense of awe and reverence. First, He will come in judgment. Then (in 11:11) He *will return them to their homes*. There is still a future for Israel because the Lord is God and not a man. He makes promises and can keep them.

And what about us? We, too, have sinned against God. If we know the Lord, we're sinning against our loving Father. And those who don't know the Lord are sinning against a God who has shown common grace. Either way, when we violate his Word, it is a personal transgression. It's a sin, whether or not we think it's right. Sin isn't up to us to define. If we had a thousand-voice choir behind us singing our innocence, we're still sinning if we're violating His Word. Sin is deceptive. It always thinks it deserved better than what it has received.

We deserve nothing but death, judgment. If you know Jesus, God has given you everything. When you respond to His Word with indifference and pursue other things, trying to replace Him with your idols, you are like an ungrateful child with a loving father who led you, cared for you and healed you. This is returning evil for good, an act of betrayal. We must not return evil for such goodness. Listen to God's voice by listening to His Word.

18
Learn from Your Past
(11:12-12:14)

The message of Hosea is drawing to a close. It will again move from indictment, to a call for repentance, to an announcement of judgment, and finally to a reminder of God's ultimate purpose, which is both gracious and hopeful.

God repeats the same message throughout the book, but always in a new way. It is as though He exhausts every available avenue in calling His people away from their sin, to a life of submission to Himself. God continues to tell the same story, since the situation hasn't changed. Yet He does so with multiplied variety. This time He calls upon them to repent and to turn to Himself, based upon their past. When people ignore God's repeated message, the guilt of a people, or an individual, increases. Present sin is often doubly inexcusable, because it's a repetition of what God had graciously dealt with in the past. There's guilt both because of the current sin, and because there has been no change in the life's pattern.

THE INDICTMENT (11:12-12:2)

So, God comes to His people, not only confronting them with their current condition, but taking them to their past via their father Jacob. From both their present and their past, He calls His people to repentance while warning them of coming judgment.

Before we can comment on this indictment, we must recognize a translation issue. The ESV has:

Hosea 11:12 *Ephraim has surrounded me with lies, and the house of Israel with deceit, but Judah still walks with God and is faithful to the Holy One* [Emphasis added].

But the NAS has:

Ephraim surrounds Me with lies, And the house of Israel with deceit; Judah is also unruly against God, Even against the Holy One who is faithful [Emphasis added].

Obviously, the Hebrew allows for it to be understood either way. The ESV sees Judah (the southern kingdom) as being faithful to God, with a remnant that *walks* with the Lord. Judah had both bad and good kings and didn't fall until 587 BC. The northern kingdom, here called *Ephraim,* had only bad kings and fell earlier, in 722 BC.

But the word רוּד (rud) translated *walks* in the ESV can also mean to wander or to roam. The NAS then sees this as Judah being *unruly* concerning God, not walking with Him. Our interpretation of this word will determine whether the word *faithful* refers to Judah.

Context is always king, and the immediate context favors the NAS. Only a couple of verses later, in **12:2**, God is bringing an indictment against Judah, the southern kingdom. It would be strange, after just saying that they are walking with You, and being faithful to You, then to say, *The LORD has an indictment against Judah and will punish Judah according to his ways.* This is not the first warning in Hosea for the southern kingdom (see 5:10; 6:4).

Even though the kingdom was split after Solomon under Rehoboam, God still deals with them in this book as one people. He's still addressing both. Hosea is usually dealing with the north, but God still has a word for His people in the south. They're both headed in the wrong direction, though at a different pace. They will be conquered at different times, but God is still warning both. Notice how He describes their sin.

Their Sin Is an Attack on God (11:12)

They sin with lies

As God describes Israel's sin, we see the true nature of sin, a personal attack against God. He pictures them as surrounding Him with lies. It's as if they have surrounded an enemy, ready to attack. Their *lies* toward the Lord, or more likely concerning the Lord, are hateful.

They sin with hypocrisy

They use *deceit*, as if they can deceive the Lord by pretending to follow Him, while surrounding Him with lies. Sin is deceptive. It likes darkness, likes to be hidden and hates light. When you live a private life of sin, with secret disobedience to God, you are attacking the living God. You have surrounded Him as though you'd surround an enemy, but it is to your own destruction. It's like saying you have a bear cornered, and all you have is your bare hands.

Proverbs 28:13 *Whoever conceals his transgressions will not prosper, but he who confesses and forsakes them will obtain mercy.*

Their Sin Is Rebellion Against Faithfulness

NAU **Hosea 11:12** *Ephraim surrounds Me with lies And the house of Israel with deceit; Judah is also unruly against God, Even against the Holy One who is faithful.*

As we saw in the last lesson, rebellion is a part of the sinfulness of sin—it is returning evil for good. Sin is hating God and attacking Him. With your sin, you're attacking the Holy God who has been nothing but faithful to you. Every day God is faithful to His creation, to His creatures, and especially faithful to His people. Because of His faithfulness, every sin is an act of betrayal and an act of rebellion, returning evil for good. It is unruliness, fighting against Him, against His Kingdom, His rule, and His person.

God is faithful, but the people of God wander from him. When we choose sin, it <u>is</u> wandering. A sinful life is an aimless life, headed nowhere. It has no true course, and nothing substantial, nothing that is lasting. It has nothing satisfying, but when you choose God your life will be purposeful, fulfilling, and will stand the test of eternity.

Their Sin Is Grasping for the Wind (12:1)

Their sin is a chasing after the wind. Though they *multiply falsehood and violence*, and though they *make a covenant* with Assyria and Egypt, it's all chasing after the wind. None of it is going to make them safe. When people pursue sin, it produces a kind of desperation. Multiplying lies is not a successful cover for sin.

People believe that THEIR story will somehow defy everything that the Bible says and warns about. Countless people have followed the same path and been destroyed for it, but they believe THEIR situation will be different!

Furthermore, they begin to reach out for help in places where they will never find help. Even their desperate and vain attempts for help are confused. Israel looks for help, alternating between two directions, taking oil to Assyria and Egypt, but it won't work. The Lord will reward according to what their deeds truly deserve, not according to what they think or claim about themselves (12:2). He has *an indictment against Judah* and will repay *Jacob according to his ways.*

AN EXAMPLE FOR REPENTANCE (12:3-6)

There is, however, a way home. The answer for them is repentance. The Lord calls them to repentance using an example from their past. He uses their forefather Jacob to represent the nation, and reminds them of three events in his life: His birth, his wrestling with the angel of the Lord, and finally a picture of him submitted to the Lord God, following the Lord's command to go to Bethel. In Jacob's life there was deception, then brokenness, and finally submission to the Lord. (In Jewish thought, the whole nation was in Jacob's loins, so Hosea can say that *there* at Bethel *God spoke with us*.)

Jacob was a deceiver from the womb (12:3)

Jacob's name meant heel-grabber. "'To grasp the heel' also meant to go behind one's back in order to deceive or trick him, and this became the dominant characteristic of the man."[15] He wanted blessing, and he was chosen for it even from the womb, reaching out to grab his brother's heel. He is pictured in his very birth providentially as a picture of the way he will get this blessing. After he stole Esau's birthright and blessing, Esau said of Jacob, *Is he not rightly named Jacob? For he has cheated me these two times. He took away my birthright, and behold, now he has taken away my blessing* (Gen. 27:36). Jacob wanted blessing, but wanted it the wrong way, finding it through deception.

Do you realize that we are all cheats from the womb? Apart from the saving work of Jesus Christ, all of us are liars and cheaters. For example, consider how people misuse and twist the facts as they try to destroy the concept of creation, making a case against God.

Jacob was changed through an encounter with God (12:3-4)

Jacob was chosen by God not only for the blessing, he was also chosen for brokenness. After cheating his brother Esau out of the blessing, Jacob fled from that country. After he married and had children and served Laban

---

[15] James Montgomery Boice, *The Minor Prophets: An Expositional Commentary (Hosea-Jonah)*. (Grand Rapids: Zondervan, 1984), en loc.

for years, Jacob headed back to his home country. On his way, Jacob wrestled throughout the night with the angel of the Lord, seeking a blessing from God (Gen. 32). It was granted to him, but not without brokenness, for he was wounded in his hip. The wound left a mark which would remain for the rest of his life. He prevailed by God's choice but was also broken as a result. This is a real point of change in Jacob's life.

Jacob learned that submission to God is the way of blessing (12:4-5)

He met God at Bethel. Again, in Jewish thought, the whole nation was in Jacob's loins, so Hosea can say, *There* (at Bethel) *God met with* **us**. This event is described in Genesis 35, where we see Jacob submitted to God, listening, obeying and following God. He has gone from deceiver, to broken, to submitted to the Lord.

Genesis 35:1 *God said to Jacob, "Arise, go up to Bethel and dwell there. Make an altar there to the God who appeared to you when you fled from your brother Esau."* *²* *So Jacob said to his household and to all who were with him, "Put away the foreign gods that are among you and purify yourselves and change your garments. ³ Then let us arise and go up to Bethel, so that I may make there an altar to the God who answers me in the day of my distress and has been with me wherever I have gone." ⁴ So they gave to Jacob all the foreign gods that they had, and the rings that were in their ears. Jacob hid them under the terebinth tree that was near Shechem. ⁵ And as they journeyed, a terror from God fell upon the cities that were around them, so that they did not pursue the sons of Jacob. ⁶ And Jacob came to Luz (that is, Bethel), which is in the land of Canaan, he and all the people who were with him, ⁷ and there he built an altar and called the place El-bethel, because there God had revealed himself to him when he fled from his brother.*

In light of their present sin, God is basically saying to Israel, "Will you learn from your father's past? Will you stop with the lies and deception? Will you be brokenhearted over what you're doing? Will you fully submit to Me so that I might demonstrate favor to you?"

A CALL TO REPENTANCE (12:6)

Verse 6 shows us that these three pictures from Jacob's life are meant to be a call to repentance. God is moving directly from a past example to their present situation. This verse is a vivid five-fold picture of repentance. If the Lord has been dealing with you concerning something in your life that's contrary to scripture, what will repentance mean? How do you return?

Make personal application of God's instruction (So you)

Repentance means you are going to make personal application of instruction from God's Word, while considering your past. In Israel's case, they are to hear it in light of what the Lord has told them about their father, Jacob, and immediately apply this lesson from the past to their lives. Repentance always involves hearing God's word, not as a vague message disconnected from your life, but as addressed personally to you. When we hear a sermon, for example, we can never stop with explanation. There must always be application: "What will this mean for my life?" Repentance is when we hear the Word of God, obediently turn from our sin and apply God's truth to our own choices, families and current situations.

Recognize your absolute need (*by the help of your God*)

We can't even repent rightly without Him. Repentance is a gift, because it's the result of God's converting work in the soul—a result of regeneration. Apart from a new heart, there cannot be a new course. But God doesn't repent for us. Repentance is synergistic. God does his work in the soul, and then man, by the grace of God, responds and lives out the fruit of that. There's a change of mind that's reflected in a change of heart and a change of course. Repentance involves living a life of step-by-step dependence on the Lord: believing His Word, depending on His ideas, not ours.

Return to the way set before us by God (*return*)

Israel needs to abandon their sin and *return* to the Lord. There must be a change of course, a whole-hearted commitment to that which God insists upon. Repentance begins in the heart, but you haven't repented if there is only a change in your emotions. You haven't repented until your behavior changes. Where there is repentance, there is a change resulting in a different way of living. There are people who say, "I love the Lord," while their entire lifestyle says just the opposite. He is near them in terms of their lips, but as the Lord said elsewhere, *their hearts are far from me* (Isaiah 29:13). The proof of repentance is found in your feet; where you walk reveals where your heart is committed.

Pursue righteousness (*hold fast to love and justice*)

Not only does repentance mean a change in course, but also a concrete commitment to pursue righteousness. Israel has been neither loving nor just. So, they must return to the Lord, hold fast, and practice what is right.

Righteousness includes basing your definition of love and justice on what God's Word says, not on what the culture says, and then living out that definition in your life. In our case, we must get rid of our culture's definitions that are based only on emotions instead of on the Bible.

Believe God's promises of blessing (*wait continually for your God*)

Besides returning to the Lord and holding fast to love and justice, Israel needs to wait for her God. Here the word *wait* carries with it the idea of hope. You wait for Him because you believe His promises of blessing, living in the light of Who He is and in what He has promised.

This wait is continual, believing God's promises of pleasure more than those of sin. "Sin is what you do when your heart is not satisfied with God."[16] God promises pleasure in <u>obedience</u>; sin promises pleasure in <u>disobedience</u>. The only way to depart from sin and walk with the Lord is to believe God, to live your life in the hope of what He's promised. If you believe that it's true, then you will follow Him, trust Him.

Think once more about Jacob. He was a cheat, but he became a broken man, and then a submitted man. Then *you*, Israel, by the help of your God, *return*, *hold fast*, and *wait continually for your God*.

THE WARNING OF CERTAIN JUSTICE (12:7-11)

But if they do not return (and of course we know they won't), the outcome has been settled. That is something that we must be convinced of in our own minds. What is set before us is life or death. There isn't the possibility of anything else. God WILL punish sin. If you won't respond to the grace of God, you'll meet with the justice of God. Verses 7-11 describe their guilt once more and warn of God's certain justice.

Sins Described (12:7-8)

The Lord describes their sins. He does this repeatedly through Hosea, because he wants us to recognize what our sin is, that we might turn from it.

---

[16] John Piper, *Future Grace, Revised Edition* (Colorado Springs: Multnomah, 2010), p. 1

Cultural conformity (12:7)

The word for *merchant* is a word that originally meant *Canaanite*. Over time, it came to mean a merchant. Here, it may actually mean Canaanite. Instead of going into the Promised Land and obeying God fully, removing the people who were characterized by these sins, the people of God were overcome by their culture. They have become Canaanites in their lifestyle, in their business dealings. They use *false balances*, and they love *to oppress*. The Lord notices how we conduct business. He cares about whether our balances are true or false, and whether we take advantage of people. If we're dishonest and oppressing people in the realm of business, it is sin. It's like a Canaanite.

We could describe their sin as cultural conformity. They look like their world, think like their world, behave like their world. And it is hateful to God.

1 John 2:15 *Do not love the world or the things in the world. If anyone loves the world, the love of the Father is not in him.* [16] *For all that is in the world—the desires of the flesh and the desires of the eyes and pride of life—is not from the Father but is from the world.* [17] *And the world is passing away along with its desires, but whoever does the will of God abides forever.*

Here, *the love of the Father is not in him* means he is not converted. And what is worldliness? Some churches make it just a list: Does a woman wear slacks? Does a man's hair touch his ears? Do you use something other than the King James Version of the Bible? No. That's not the meaning of worldliness in the Bible. It's following *the desires of the flesh and the desires of the eyes and pride of life*. It's a flesh-driven, self-driven, material-possession-driven life. It's living a life with ambitions that are not those set forth for God's people by God. We're to live in light of our King and His Kingdom and eternity. If your life is temporally driven, that's living like the world.

Compromised conscience (12:8)

The Lord has just specified their sin, but they can no longer see their sin. They think of themselves as just good businesspeople. *Ah, but I am rich.* They claim that they are doing nothing wrong. *In all my labors they cannot find in me iniquity or sin.* God is revealing their hearts. They are in the midst of sin, but they can't see it. They're claiming innocence, but they are about to face judgment for how they're living.

People may claim to be doing no wrong, but that means nothing. Our thinking, our words and our behavior must all be measured by Scripture. If the Bible reveals it to be sinful, it's sinful. There is a sad progression, beginning with lies, then more lies to cover them up. Finally, they actually believe their own lies and become bolder in their sinning. The conscience can be seared (1 Timothy 4:2). These people have arrived at the place where they deny the very sin that God is confronting. So, they're not repenting, because they don't think they have anything to repent of. But what does the Lord say to them?

Judgment Promised (12:9-11)

The Lord tells them that judgment is coming. We can organize what He's saying around three questions.

Do you not fear God? (12:9)

God says, *I am the* LORD *your God from the land of Egypt.* It's like an introduction. He reminds them of Who He is and of what He's done. They think they are wealthy, but He will make them *dwell in tents once more as in the days of the appointed feast*—the Feast of Booths, celebrating how God took care of them in their wilderness wanderings after they left Egypt. He led them out, but He's able to take them from their land of richness back to living in tents. It's as if he is asking them, "Have you forgotten Who I am?"

Do you not hear the prophets? (12:10)

They say they have no iniquity, but where do they think these prophetic messages are coming from? God says they came from Him. He *spoke to the prophets.* He *multiplied visions.* He gave them the *parables* they've spoken, and in some cases, in the case of Hosea and Gomer's marriage, lived before them. This was coming from the Lord.

Do you not realize what God wants? (12:11)

What He wants is righteousness. *If there is iniquity in Gilead, they shall surely come to nothing*—and this is how the people constantly try to deal with their problems: *in Gilgal they sacrifice bulls*, but God is going to tear down their altars. They will be *like stone heaps on the furrows of the field*. He will wipe out their altars.

The Lord doesn't want their sacrifices. Instead, as we saw in verse 6, He wants them to return to Him, by His help. He wants them to hold fast to love and justice, to put away their false balances, to stop oppressing people, and to stop living like the peoples around them, because God's people are not Canaanites. He doesn't want their religion. He wants their life.

AN EXAMPLE FOR REVERENCE (12:12-14)

Humble beginnings (12:12)

In this verse, He again reminds them of their humble beginnings, when *Jacob fled* from Esau *to the land of Aram* and had to serve there *for a wife*. He was only a shepherd.

Holy grace (12:13)

In verse 10, the Lord reminded them that these messages have been coming through prophets. Now He emphasizes that it was by a prophet (Moses) that He brought Israel up out of Egypt, and it was by a prophet that Israel was guarded. They had humble beginnings, but they were blessed. The Lord was their deliverer and their provider. Prophets were present for deliverance and protection, not judgment. But if they won't listen, they will be humble again—this time, not as a blessing, but as discipline. The prophets will not be deliverers and guardians for them, but instruments of God's judgment—and this is, in fact, where they are headed.

Disgraceful return (12:14)

Ephraim has given bitter provocation. As a result, *his Lord will leave his bloodguilt on him and will repay him for his disgraceful deeds.* Their actions have been bitter provocation to the Lord, doubly disgraceful: disgraceful in their essence and disgraceful in view of all the Lord has done for them.

APPLYING IT

Can you learn from your past?

Don't be like Israel. Can you hear the Lord speaking to you about His faithfulness, and about how often and how deeply you have rebelled? If you won't be benefited by instruction, you will be reproved by iniquity. Sin is never rewarded with blessing. Your case will be no different.

Are you listening to Him?

Do you hear Him challenging your sin? Do you hear Him willingly, or do you claim that you have no sins?

Are you really repentant?

When you come back around to another opportunity to make the same choice, just in different clothes, will you now make the right decision? A true test of your spiritual condition is whether you can benefit from instruction from God. When the Lord gives you a warning, presenting you with lessons from the past in Scripture, bringing you face to face with your own past failures and departures from the right standard, and then gives another opportunity, will you take a different course?

What will you do with a book like Hosea? Will you listen, return, hold fast, love justice, and wait continually for the Lord?

19
The Autopsy of a Nation
(13:1-16)

There is more than one kind of death. This was clearly witnessed in the garden when Adam fell. The Lord God told them that they would die in the day that they ate of the fruit.

Genesis 2:17 *but of the tree of the knowledge of good and evil you shall not eat, for in the day that you eat of it you shall surely die."*

They ate, and they died, but their death had more than one aspect. They experienced a <u>spiritual death</u> immediately. Something clearly changed. Their relationships to sin, to purity, to themselves, and to God and to each other all changed.

Sin brought separation from God, shown by their attempt to hide themselves from the Lord.

Genesis 3:7 *Then the eyes of both were opened, and they knew that they were naked. And they sewed fig leaves together and made themselves loincloths. ⁸ And they heard the sound of the Lord God walking in the garden in the cool of the day, and the man and his wife hid themselves from the presence of the Lord God among the trees of the garden. ⁹ But the Lord God called to the man and said to him, "Where are you?" ¹⁰ And he said, "I heard the sound of you in the garden, and I was afraid, because I was naked, and I hid myself." ¹¹ He said, "Who told you that you were naked? Have you eaten of the tree of which I commanded you not to eat?"*

It was also immediately evident that their relationship to each other had changed. They became aware that they were naked, and they clothed themselves, but this clothing was unacceptable to God. He demonstrated the Gospel by clothing them through the death of an animal, which pictures sacrifice. They began to blame each other and to blame God. After they were expelled from the garden, it wasn't long before Cain murdered his brother Abel. <u>Spiritual death</u> was now being put on display in kind of a social death, sinful behavior. Many years later, Adam and Eve themselves experienced the <u>physical death</u> that they were promised from the beginning if they disobeyed the Lord.

This same pattern is repeated again and again in the world since the fall, though not from the point of innocence that Adam and Eve knew originally. There is a pattern of good beginnings, spiritual decisions that initiate decline, the social decay that accompanies the slide, and finally the physical end toward which the decay was headed.

This is seen here in Hosea 13. We could describe this chapter as a spiritual autopsy. Israel has died, only the death hasn't finished its course yet. The Lord declares the death of the kingdom, both describing and explaining it.

A DESCRIPTION OF ISRAEL'S DEATH (13:1-3)

Spiritual Death (13:1)

A Place of Favor and Respect

The tribe of Ephraim is considered here as a representative for what has happened with the entire nation. Of Joseph's sons, it was Ephraim who was given the place of prominence over his brother Manasseh. In Genesis 48:1-20 you can read about Jacob's blessing of Ephraim, the younger son of Joseph, instead of Manasseh, the older. Since that time, it is the tribe of Ephraim that had the greatest influence in the North.

> When Ephraim, the most powerful tribe, spoke early in Israel's history; it was with authority and produced fear. – John MacArthur[17]

---

[17] John MacArthur, *The MacArthur Bible Commentary,* 1 vol., pg. 980

The picture of Ephraim is one of prominence, favor, blessing and privilege.

A Fall

The nation of Israel will fall due to idolatry and a commitment to Baal worship. There was a conscious decision to choose the way of the surrounding culture, instead of the way set before them by God. And in that choice not to believe God, but to believe and pursue a lie instead, a spiritual death occurred.

> The prophet recalls the days past when Ephraim was honored in the nation. When he spoke, all trembled; men had respect for his power and prestige. One can hardly read the history of the twelve tribes without noting how prominent was the position of Ephraim. He was truly exalted in Israel, respectfully feared. But when he gave himself over to the worship of Baal under Ahab (1 Kings 16:31), he died. His power was destroyed and broken. He died spiritually with consequent political decline. —Charles Feinberg[18]

Idolatry among the people of God, both in the northern and southern kingdoms, predated their actual fall and captivity by many years. If Feinberg is right to identify this choice of death with Ahab, it was about 150 years from the nation's spiritual death to its physical finish. In other words, the spiritual death and the guilt incurred through idolatry, preceded the actual physical destruction of the nation.

For all those years, Israel was dead; they just didn't know it yet. They were dead, even while they were living out the remaining years allowed by God, to enjoy in the land.

Social Decay (13:2)

Notice that the spiritual death in the nation manifests itself in social decay. We're not to have anything before the Lord. Idolatry is not just the worship of physical images. We can make idols in our minds by not honoring God as God, or not thinking about God as we ought, or putting something

---

[18] Charles Feinberg, *The Minor Prophets*, pg. 63

or someone else in the place of God. This is what a life looks like when we choose sin and disobedience to the Lord.

Idolatry results in:

- **Wasted pursuits**—Sin is a downhill road. Man was created to find his satisfaction in God. Where there's genuine fellowship with the true and living God, the heart is satisfied. There is joy, purpose, meaning and peace. Idolatry, in all its forms, is an insatiable appetite, resulting in humanity moving from one form of sin to more and more extreme forms.

- **Wasted treasure**—They take valuable materials and waste them in the construction of gods they have made and bow down to them. These precious resources are being wasted on gods that are not really gods. Remember the prodigal son who leaves his father and goes off to pursue his life of sin. He takes the treasure that had been set aside for him by his father and wastes it all in sinful living. That's the picture of a sinful life and wasted treasure.

- **Wasted talents**—Hosea stresses the thought, care and the skill that has been invested in their idolatry. The craftsmen are taking their talents that ought to be used for the glory of the true God, and investing them in making these images.

  God has put abilities within each one of us, that are meant to be used unto His glory. When you take your mind and your hands, and the skills that you have, and waste them in sin, that's idolatry. It's vain—empty.

- **Wasted dignity**—*It is said of them, "Those who offer human sacrifice kiss calves!"* Literally, the Hebrew is something like this: <u>*sacrificers of men*</u>. It could be taken to refer to human sacrifice, but it also can be taken to mean <u>sacrificers among men</u>. There's no evidence that Baal worship at this time involves human sacrifice. It is likely Hosea is saying this: Those among men who are offering these sacrifices have been kissing these images formed by their own hands.

That man, who was made a little lower than the angels, would stoop to kiss the image of a calf, is man throwing away the very dignity that God placed upon him. He was given lordship over the creation and granted, by God's grace and mercy, this place of privilege and honor among His creatures. However, due to unbelief and sin, we are reduced to kissing the work of our own fingers.

Today, those who endorse the theory of evolution, are fighting for the idea that there is nothing unique about man. While noting some differences, they believe it is just a matter of chance, nothing a Creator would have done. They fight to take away our own place of privilege and dignity given to us by God. Man will willingly denigrate himself in the pursuit of sin.

Sudden Destruction (13:3)

Here God uses four clearly understood images (*mist, dew, chaff* and *smoke*) to convey the temporary nature of their existence as a nation. Physical destruction will follow and is the consequence of their spiritual death.

AN EXPLANATION FOR ISRAEL'S DEATH (13:4-6)

How does this happen? How do people live such wasteful lives?

A Willful Rejection of God's Self-Revelation (13:4)

In verses 4-6 God explains Israel's death. He begins by referring to Exodus, chapter 20, the beginning of the Ten Commandments.

Exodus 20:2 *"I am the LORD your God, who brought you out of the land of Egypt, out of the house of slavery. ³ "You shall have no other gods before me. ⁴ "You shall not make for yourself a carved image, or any likeness of anything that is in heaven above, or that is in the earth beneath, or that is in the water under the earth. ⁵ You shall not bow down to them or serve them, for I the LORD your God am a jealous God, visiting the iniquity of the fathers on the children to the third and the fourth generation of those who hate me, ⁶ but showing steadfast love to thousands of those who love me and keep my commandments.*

God is reminding them of what He has told them. To enter into this Baal worship, they had to willfully reject prophets like Moses and Hosea. Israel has also rejected God's Word (such as the Ten Commandments) that came through these prophets.

They also had to reject and to forget God's powerful deeds throughout the history and the life of the nation that should have kept their hearts tied to the one true and living God. He says, *But I am the Lord your God from the land of Egypt.* How were they delivered from Egypt? All the plagues that the Lord sent were undeniable evidence of His existence and His activity with them. But they willfully reject all of that and decide to worship Baal, even to the point that now they're kissing the work of their own hands.

A Willful Forgetting of God's Gracious Provision (13:5-6)

Israel has forgotten how God provided for them in the past, when they were in the wilderness and when they entered the Promised Land. They are proud, self-confident, independent and self-sufficient. They have forgotten their God.

THE RESULT OF ISRAEL'S DEATH (13:7-16)

The Lord has described their death, and now He details its result. The first, seen in vs. 1-6, is that by rejecting God, they have forfeited their place of blessing, high honor and favor, choosing to follow their own gods.

God Becomes Israel's Enemy

Israel is now *against* the Lord (:9). They will be <u>judged with great fierceness</u> (:7-8) like that of wild animals. Each animal mentioned is native to the area in Hosea's day, so the people can certainly understand him. I remember a trip to South Africa to visit a seminary. We traveled through areas with wild animals and were instructed not even to get out of the car. One day there was a report of someone who had been traveling on foot and was eaten by a lion. The Lord says in verse 7, *I am to them like a lion; like a leopard I will lurk beside the way.* He will fall on them *like a bear robbed of her cubs.* He will *tear open their breast* and *devour them like a lion.* Those are not tame words. The Lord is not the safe god who is always "inspirational." He gets angry with sin. He hates it. He works to destroy it.

They will also be <u>left without help</u> (:9) because they chose the decay of sin. They are now related to God, not as a friend, but as an enemy.

Hosea 13:9 *He destroys you, O Israel, for you are against me, against your helper.*

He destroys you can be translated *I will destroy* you, as in the NET Bible and the CSB. When you are against your only helper, then what's left for you is destruction. Notice that God is active in this. One thing you will not find in the Bible is the idea that God only works to save people, but never to destroy people. When you set yourself against the Lord, He is not your savior, He is your judge, and He judges sin.

God Mocks Their Foolish Desires (13:10-11)

Israel wanted to be like the other nations, with a king, instead of being ruled by the Lord. They thought this would be the answer to all their problems, but God's question is, *Where now is your king to save you in all your cities?* When God is judging a people, He often demonstrates their foolishness by asking this kind of question. The same attitude of rebellion is seen today when people explain their nation's greatness by looking to themselves—their ingenuity, their persistence, their courage, their bright minds, their prosperity, their wise leaders. They can no longer see that every blessing comes by the grace of God. He gave it, and He can take it away.

This is not the only place in the Bible where mocking is found. The Lord, through Elijah, mocked the prophets of Baal.

1 Kings 18:27 *And at noon Elijah mocked them, saying, "Cry aloud, for he is a god. Either he is musing, or he is relieving himself, or he is on a journey, or perhaps he is asleep and must be awakened."*

Through Jeremiah, God mocked Israel about their idols:

Jeremiah 2:26 *"As a thief is shamed when caught, so the house of Israel shall be shamed: they, their kings, their officials, their priests, and their prophets,* ²⁷ *who say to a tree, 'You are my father,' and to a stone, 'You gave me birth.' For they have turned their back to me, and not their face. But in the time of their trouble they say, 'Arise and save us!'* ²⁸ *But where are your gods that you made for yourself? Let them arise, if they can save you, in your time of trouble; for as many as your cities are your gods, O Judah."*

People today examine jellyfish, trying to find clues about how we got our beginning. They are like those *who say to a tree, "You are my father."*

They Will Be Held Accountable for All Their Sin (13:12)

God hasn't forgotten any of their sin. It's *bound up, kept in store,* and they will face the penalty.

They Are Being Reminded of Their Unwillingness to Repent (13:13)

God has given them opportunities to repent, over and over again, which makes this stubbornness painful and unnecessary. He pictures this as a child that is in the process of being born but is unwilling to come out. Israel is refusing to repent and be reborn.

They Won't Be Rescued, but Will Be Severely Punished (13:14-16)

There's a debate about how to understand the two questions, *O Death, where are your plagues? O Sheol, where is your sting?* This is because it is quoted in the New Testament as a promise of resurrection. Emphasis is placed on the fact that for believers, death no longer has a sting. But the immediate context here makes very clear these are not compassionate statements from God, but ones of condemnation. He says, *Compassion is hidden from my eyes.* We could translate the first two lines of verse 14 as questions: *Shall I ransom them from the power of Sheol? Shall I redeem them from death?* He is beckoning the sting of death to fall upon them. When these verses are quoted in the New Testament, emphasis is placed on the fact that for believers, death and Sheol no longer have a sting. There are no plagues left for believers, because God poured out His wrath on His own Son in our place, if we trust Christ. There is no judgment of condemnation left for us, because our sins have been judged at the tree.

Finally, we see the severity of the punishment. At the time when Hosea is ministering, they are just coming out of one of the greatest times of prosperity and expansion that the nation has ever known. They seem to *flourish among* their *brothers* (13:15). It is likely they cannot imagine that their fortunes will be taken away and will not save them. But Hosea's hearers won't be delivered. They ought not even dream that they will be. The Lord's judgment will be like a desert *wind*, drying up their *fountains* (that is, their source of life). The Lord is telling them not to imagine that they will be saved by their prosperity. He will take it all away.

The horrific acts described in verse 16 will have a literal fulfillment in 722 BC when the cruel Assyrians take them away.

APPLYING IT

Chapter 13 of Hosea has been full of bad news. The good news is that when we trust in Christ, all the kinds of judgment and punishment we've seen toward Israel will be reversed. Blessing is not forfeited—it begins in Christ. God is not our judge, but our friend. Even when we fall, there isn't mocking for our failures. There is comfort, encouragement, rescue and change. Have you been running after things that will never satisfy your heart? Life and death are set before you. Each of us will either meet with God on the ground of grace as our Lord and Savior or will meet with Him on the ground of judgment as judge and destroyer.

Matthew 3:11 *"I baptize you with water for repentance, but he who is coming after me is mightier than I, whose sandals I am not worthy to carry. He will baptize you with the Holy Spirit and fire. ¹² His winnowing fork is in his hand, and he will clear his threshing floor and gather his wheat into the barn, but the chaff he will burn with unquenchable fire."*

Revelation 6:15 *Then the kings of the earth and the great ones and the generals and the rich and the powerful, and everyone, slave and free, hid themselves in the caves and among the rocks of the mountains, ¹⁶ calling to the mountains and rocks, "Fall on us and hide us from the face of him who is seated on the throne, and from the wrath of the Lamb, ¹⁷ for the great day of their wrath has come, and who can stand?"*

Revelation 14:9 *And another angel, a third, followed them, saying with a loud voice, "If anyone worships the beast and its image and receives a mark on his forehead or on his hand, ¹⁰ he also will drink the wine of God's wrath, poured full strength into the cup of his anger, and he will be tormented with fire and sulfur in the presence of the holy angels and in the presence of the Lamb. ¹¹ And the smoke of their torment goes up forever and ever, and they have no rest, day or night, these worshipers of the beast and its image, and whoever receives the mark of its name." ¹² Here is a call for the endurance of the saints, those who keep the commandments of God and their faith in Jesus. ¹³ And I heard a voice from heaven saying, "Write this: Blessed are the dead who die in the Lord from now on." "Blessed indeed," says the Spirit, "that they may rest from their labors, for their deeds follow them!"*

Will the presence of Christ mean comfort for you, or torment?

20
Coming Home
(14:1-3)

God has a specific goal in mind as He uses Hosea to communicate His Word. The main message in this book has been God confronting Israel with their sin and warning of judgment. He declares certain disaster because they refuse to repent. The Lord, through the prophet, is bringing His people face-to-face with their sins and calling upon them to recognize how grave and destructive those sins are. But He doesn't want Israel to just recognize that they have sinned, nor even to recognize where all that sin is leading them. He urges them to recognize it so that they'll be rescued from it. Interspersed throughout the book are unmistakable pictures of God's love, His amazing patience, and His grace. He calls for them to turn from sin to Himself, to the living God—to receive His forgiveness and to submit their lives to Him. That's the goal of the book of Hosea, and it becomes clearer as we look at God's final word to them—as we look at where the book ends.

Hosea ends with a message of hope and of grace. Not only is there a closing call for repentance and a closing description of repentance; there's also a closing promise of repentance. We'll examine this more in the next lesson, but notice that in verses 4-7, He promises to heal their apostasy and to love them freely with His anger having turned away from them. He promises them prosperity and fame. Before we get to that, let's look at God's call for repentance.

THE CALL TO REPENTANCE (14:1)

God calls Israel to repentance by inviting and commanding them to return to Him because they have stumbled due to their iniquity. The question,

"How do you return to the Lord?" is an important one. If you don't know Christ as your Savior, and are not reconciled to God, you're a sinner by nature and have become a sinner by choice. You are outside the loving fellowship of the living God, and you should be asking, "How do I get to the Lord?" And for those who do know the Lord, but who are not walking obediently with Him right now, maybe you've run so far from Him that you wonder, "How do I get back?" Let the Lord speak to you through this passage. As we look at this verse, at this call to repentance, we can observe three aspects of the nature of repentance.

Repentance Is a Personal Return to God

Repentance is not just a commitment to a new way. It's a fresh commitment to the Lord God Himself. Israel is to *return* to a person, to *the Lord*. In a right relationship to God, there is a personal relationship. He is not just the Lord God; He is OUR Lord and God. He is my God, my Ruler, my King, and my Sovereign. He is the goal of my life and the joy of my heart and the reason for my living.

Repentance Includes a Personal Recognition of Sin Before God

Why does Israel, and why do we, need to return to the Lord? Israel must recognize that they have *stumbled* because of their *iniquity*. They have sinned against the Lord. They can't turn to the Lord unless they acknowledge their sin. Then they will recognize that the devastation in their land is due to their iniquity.

- Repentance is recognizing that we have been in the wrong place: We have *stumbled*.
- Repentance is recognizing the cause of that wrong place: It is *because of* our *iniquity*. Iniquity (עָוֺן, avon) is a strong word meaning crooked, twisted, perverted. It's not just a mistake or some small mess-up. Before we repent, we usually minimize our sin and are often absolutely blind to how our sin has produced our troubles. Where there's real repentance, our sin is not small in our own view. It seems to be the largest thing in the world. The things that once seemed like small sins to us now make us shudder.

Repentance Is Answering the Call of God

It's not just Hosea calling Israel to repentance. God is calling through him. God initiates our repentance and calls to us to leave our sin. He calls us to trust Him, to submit to Him and to rest in Him. We hear the Lord through His Word, and we respond.

THE PICTURE OF REPENTANCE (14:2-3)

We now have a picture of repentance, and it is amazing to remember that these are the Lord's words. It is as though God Himself is taking the nation of Israel by the hand and telling her what to do, what to say, and what to believe—telling Israel how to repent.

Repentance Requires Humble Confession

It's interesting that the first thing He tells them is not to bring sacrifices, but to bring *words* to *the Lord*. This is a clear picture of humble confession. As the entire Old Testament makes plain, God takes no delight in empty words. If we bring only empty words, it's not repentance. He calls us to bring the sincere fruit of our heart. What comes immediately to mind is Jesus' story of another son who took words to his father.

Luke 15:17 *"But when he came to himself, he said, 'How many of my father's hired servants have more than enough bread, but I perish here with hunger!* [18] *I will arise and go to my father, and I will say to him, "Father, I have sinned against heaven and before you.* [19] *I am no longer worthy to be called your son. Treat me as one of your hired servants." '* [20] *And he arose and came to his father. But while he was still a long way off, his father saw him and felt compassion, and ran and embraced him and kissed him.* [21] *And the son said to him, 'Father, I have sinned against heaven and before you. I am no longer worthy to be called your son.' "*

He has given thought to what he will say, and it is the honest expression of his heart. If we are to return to the Lord, we must bring words to Him, heart-felt words showing our agreement with what God has said about our sin.

Repentance Requires Earnest Prayer

Repentance also requires earnest prayer asking forgiveness. Israel needs to recognize the scope and enormity of their sins, asking God to take them all away. They not only want to be forgiven, but there's also a willingness to have those sins removed from their behavior. They then will be ready to offer the Lord their obedience and worship, fulfilling the vows of their lips.

Repentance Requires Surrender and Dependence

Israel will no longer try to take care of herself by trusting in things other than God. They will have recognized their sins, and they will turn from them. Returning to the Lord means there will be no more reliance on foreign help or their own military strength. Finished with idolatry, they will no longer say, *Our God* to what they have made.

Repentance Seeks Mercy

Israel has now placed themselves in a position where there is no one favorable to them because of their own sin, disobedience and stubbornness. They are alone, orphaned, and call out to God for mercy. He has declared Himself to be the God who has compassion on widows and orphans. This is the character of their God. Who would love an orphan like Israel? Only God.

APPLYING IT

Just as Israel needs to turn specifically from reliance on Assyria, from their reliance on their own military, and from worshiping the Baals, so you and I must turn from our specific sin. Whatever it is that we know is wrong, wherever we have sinned against the Lord, we need to turn from that very sin and know that He has mercy for orphans.

21
Israel's Salvation and Ours
(14:4-9)

The book of Hosea ends with the promise of salvation. From the very beginning, when you see Hosea purchasing back for himself his unfaithful wife, Gomer, there is the message of pity, mercy, grace and salvation. The northern and southern kingdoms will be disciplined severely, taken away into captivity. They will suffer at the hands of Gentile nations who will serve the purpose of the true God. Even though they don't acknowledge Him, they will be His instruments to discipline His wayward children. But God will not cast them away forever. What takes place over the course of history has a redemptive purpose. In the end, God will fulfill all the promises He made to their fathers. This means that the nation's restoration will not be explained by the nation, but by God.

Remember that salvation's story is the story of God, whether it is the salvation of Israel or that of believers today. All salvation is a story about God.

If you are not a Jew, remember God's warning in Romans 11:25-36. Salvation has been poured out among Gentiles (non-Jews), and God is gathering many, many of them in faith toward the Lord Jesus Christ. Today, most of the Jewish nation has rejected its Messiah in unbelief. But God warns us Gentiles about arrogance. Salvation isn't about Jews and Gentiles. At its root, it's about Him.

God is saying that for ethnic Israel, there's still a plan of future salvation, but it won't be apart from individual salvation. Every Israelite who will ever be saved, will be saved through faith in Jesus Christ. Just as God is pouring out salvation upon Gentiles today, one day He will again pour out salvation upon ethnic Israelites.

Both through people's unbelief and through salvation, God is demonstrating that salvation is not due to any human goodness. Both Jews and Gentiles have sinned and come short of His glory. All are sinners deserving of wrath, unbelievers by nature. They all need God's mercy, grace and salvation in His Son.

Romans 11:25 *Lest you be wise in your own sight, I want you to understand this mystery, brothers: a partial hardening has come upon Israel, until the fullness of the Gentiles has come in. *[26]* And in this way all Israel will be saved, as it is written, "The Deliverer will come from Zion, he will banish ungodliness from Jacob"; *[27]* "and this will be my covenant with them when I take away their sins." *[28]* As regards the gospel, they are enemies of God for your sake. But as regards election, they are beloved for the sake of their forefathers. *[29]* For the gifts and the calling of God are irrevocable. *[30]* For just as you were at one time disobedient to God but now have received mercy because of their disobedience, *[31]* so they too have now been disobedient in order that by the mercy shown to you they also may now receive mercy. *[32]* For God has consigned all to disobedience, that he may have mercy on all. *[33]* Oh, the depth of the riches and wisdom and knowledge of God! How unsearchable are his judgments and how inscrutable his ways! *[34]* "For who has known the mind of the Lord, or who has been his counselor?" *[35]* "Or who has given a gift to him that he might be repaid?" *[36]* For from him and through him and to him are all things. To him be glory forever. Amen.*

The book of Hosea ends with a promise of the future salvation of Israel. Israel's story is always the same, the story of the gracious and true God.

GOD WILL BRING THEM TO LASTING REPENTANCE (14:4)

Repentance is a necessity, and the Lord will not grant salvation apart from it. Yet Israel, like the rest of mankind, has proven incapable of repentance. The first *I will* in this passage involves a change in their hearts. For God to give the results, He must grant the necessary conditions. Repentance is not God's response to some human work, to people bringing the right attitude, words and deeds to Him. Instead, God says HE will heal their apostasy. HE will stop their turning away from Him.

God will not save someone and leave them in a rebellious state. Where there is genuine repentance, there is always faith. Penitent faith is a gift from God. So, there's no salvation apart from repentance and faith.

God is the one who produces repentance in man, then man offers repentance, but it's a gift from God. The Bible presents us with what may seem like a paradox, but it's not. It's explained by the Lord.

Man Is Responsible for His Heart Condition

First, the Bible is clear that man is responsible for his heart condition. We are born haters of God and are responsible for being haters of God, due to the sin of our father, Adam. He was created in an innocent state and given a command by God, which he disobeyed. That's where man fell and where our natures were all corrupted. We are responsible for it because we were all represented by Adam. We were in Adam, and when he fell, we all fell. We're all responsible for this in him.

Zechariah tells us why God is angry with Israel: It's because they willingly hardened their hearts toward Him even though He revealed His will to them.

Zechariah 7:12 *They made their hearts diamond-hard lest they should hear the law and the words that the LORD of hosts had sent by his Spirit through the former prophets. Therefore great anger came from the LORD of hosts.*

This is echoed in the New Testament.

Romans 2:5 *But because of your hard and impenitent heart you are storing up wrath for yourself on the day of wrath when God's righteous judgment will be revealed.*

God Commands Man to Have a Changed Heart Condition

Not only is man responsible for his heart condition, but God commands men to change their heart condition.

Ezekiel 18:31 *Cast away from you all the transgressions that you have committed, and make yourselves a new heart and a new spirit! Why will you die, O house of Israel?*

Even more plainly:

Deuteronomy 10:16 *Circumcise therefore the foreskin of your heart, and be no longer stubborn.*

Sinful Man Is Incapable of Obeying Those Commands

This may seem like a paradox, because although you're responsible for your heart condition, and God commands you to change it, you can't change it, not by yourself.

Jeremiah 13:23 *Can the Ethiopian change his skin or the leopard his spots? Then also you can do good who are accustomed to do evil.*

God Must Grant What God Commands

God's promises to restore Israel involve promises to do an internal work. Since Israel is incapable of changing her heart by herself, God Himself must produce the change.

Ezekiel 11:19 *And I will give them one heart, and a new spirit I will put within them. I will remove the heart of stone from their flesh and give them a heart of flesh,*

Jeremiah 24:7 *I will give them a heart to know that I am the LORD, and they shall be my people and I will be their God, for they shall return to me with their whole heart.*

Jeremiah 32:39 *I will give them one heart and one way, that they may fear me forever, for their own good and the good of their children after them.*

Ezekiel 36:26 *And I will give you a new heart, and a new spirit I will put within you. And I will remove the heart of stone from your flesh and give you a heart of flesh.*

Deuteronomy 30:6 *And the LORD your God will circumcise your heart and the heart of your offspring, so that you will love the LORD your God with all your heart and with all your soul, that you may live.*

Circumcision of the heart doesn't happen by law-keeping, but by the work of the Holy Spirit.

Romans 2:29 *But a Jew is one inwardly, and circumcision is a matter of the heart, by the Spirit, not by the letter. His praise is not from man but from God.*

Man May Cry Out to God for This Work

The Bible also teaches that man may cry out to the Lord to do this work in his heart. David writes:

Psalm 51:10 *Create in me a clean heart, O God, and renew a right spirit within me.*

GOD WILL LOVE THEM GRACIOUSLY (14:4)

God has loved Israel and will forgive her with a love that is gracious. The Hebrew word translated *freely* (נְדָבָה nə·dā·ḇāh) comes from a root that speaks of something voluntary. The idea is something generous and free. This is the story of God's love and grace toward mankind.

The question we must face as soon as we believe the doctrine of election is: God, why have you loved me and chosen me for salvation?

It Is Not Because We Have Loved Him

There are a several possibilities for why God has loved us, but none of them include our loving Him. According to the Scriptures, that's not salvation's story.

1 John 4:10 *In this is love, not that we have loved God but that he loved us and sent his Son to be the propitiation for our sins.*

1 John 4:19 *We love because he first loved us.*

Romans 5:8 *but God shows his love for us in that while we were still sinners, Christ died for us.*

It Is Not Because We Are Lovely

Perhaps, we think, God has loved us because we are lovely, but that's not what we find in the scriptures. We are born evildoers, filthy and weak, but here's the wonderful good news of the gospel. God regarded us for what we really were when He took the steps to save us. He wasn't deceived about our true nature, thinking He was saving good people. Christ died for sinners, for the ungodly.

Isaiah 64:6 *We have all become like one who is unclean, and all our righteous deeds are like a polluted garment. We all fade like a leaf, and our iniquities, like the wind, take us away.*

Revelation 22:11 *"Let the evildoer still do evil, and the filthy still be filthy, and the righteous still do right, and the holy still be holy."*

Romans 5:6 *For while we were still weak, at the right time Christ died for the ungodly. ⁷ For one will scarcely die for a righteous person—though perhaps for a good* *person one would dare even to die— ⁸ but God shows his love for us in that while we were still sinners, Christ died for us.*

It Is Not Because of Some Greatness We Possess

Maybe God will save Israel because of some greatness they possessed—talent, wisdom, goodness, lifestyle. He goes all the way back to Abraham and says, in effect, "You know why I'm taking you out of Egypt? It's because of promises I made to Abraham and Isaac and Jacob. Those promises were free-grace promises. They never deserved or earned them. No, God has not loved them because they are so great. He's loved them because He's loved them.

Deuteronomy 7:6 *"For you are a people holy to the LORD your God. The LORD your God has chosen you to be a people for his treasured possession, out of all the peoples who are on the face of the earth. ⁷ It was not because you were more in number than any other people that the LORD set his love on you and chose you, for you were the fewest of all peoples, ⁸ but it is because the LORD loves you and is keeping the oath that he swore to your fathers, that the LORD has brought you out with a mighty hand and redeemed you from the house of slavery, from the hand of Pharaoh king of Egypt."*

It Is Not Because of Some Need in God

Another possible reason for God's love toward man is that He had a need to love. He was lonely, wanting fellowship and some need was met by loving us. In Deuteronomy 10:14-15, we see that is absolutely not true. Notice the word *yet*. Even though God needs nothing, He has loved you. His love for you is not explained by what He needs. He needs nothing.

Deuteronomy 10:14 *Behold, to the LORD your God belong heaven and the heaven of heavens, the earth with all that is in it. ¹⁵ Yet the LORD set his heart in love on your fathers and chose their offspring after them, you above all peoples, as you are this day.*

Never forget, there was perfect love and fellowship in the Godhead before there was any created thing. When Jesus prays for us in John 17, He celebrates at the same time this love that He's had with the Father from all eternity.

John 17:20 *"I do not ask for these only, but also for those who will believe in me through their word, ²¹ that they may all be one, just as you, Father, are in me, and I in you, that they also may be in us, so that the world may believe that you have sent me. ²² The glory that you have given me I have given to them, that they may be one even as we are one, ²³ I in them and you in me, that they may become perfectly one, so that the world may know that you sent me and loved them even as you loved me. ²⁴ Father, I desire that* *they also, whom you have given me, may be with me where I am, to see my glory that you have given me because you loved me before the foundation of the world. ²⁵ O righteous Father, even though the world does not know you, I know you, and these know that you have sent me. ²⁶ I made known to them your name, and I will continue to make it known, that the love with which you have loved me may be in them, and I in them."*

We can eliminate every conceivable explanation for God's love, but one. It is explained by His own free will. It is not obligatory, but voluntary and free. God will love them graciously and freely, not because they deserve it, but because it was His choice.

GOD HAS BEEN PROPITIATED CONCERNING THEM (14:4)

There's a third aspect of salvation's story. God's anger has turned away from them. He has been propitiated. God can do this work of salvation because justice has been satisfied. But how has it been satisfied?

Does God look at the nation of Israel sometime in the future and say, "Well, it's because they've suffered enough. They've paid for their sins"?

Or perhaps God has forgotten about their sins—how stubborn, rebellious, and idolatrous they've been. Somewhere in the future God will sort of just lose His anger. But that would be contrary to His promise of chapter 13, verse 12. He says, *The iniquity of Ephraim is bound up; his sin is kept in store.* God will preserve it in His remembrance because He's going to punish it.

Maybe they've earned this new attitude from God. Through their repentance and their different living, now God will not be angry with them because they've changed their ways. But that wouldn't correspond with His declaration of love. He says, "I've loved them graciously." Such forgiveness wouldn't be gracious, but something they earned.

We <u>know</u> how. God's anger has been satisfied, and it is not for any of these reasons. We see it illustrated from the beginning of human history. God's anger is taken away only through a propitiatory sacrifice, only through the work of redemption, and only by the blood of His Lamb. It is through the death of the innocent one, the divine substitute, the Lamb of God. God's anger will be turned away from this people, but not apart from a just answer for their sins.

This future day of salvation will be centered on the Lord Jesus Christ. This salvation will be done through individuals. Notice that each household will mourn.

Zechariah 12:10 *"And I will pour out on the house of David and the inhabitants of Jerusalem a spirit of grace and pleas for mercy, so that, when they look on me, on him whom they have pierced, they shall mourn for him, as one mourns for an only child, and weep bitterly over him, as one weeps over a firstborn.* *11 On that day the mourning in Jerusalem will be as great as the mourning for Hadad-rimmon in the plain of Megiddo. 12 The land shall mourn, each family by itself: the family of the house of David by itself, and their wives by themselves; the family of the house of Nathan by itself, and their wives by themselves; 13 the family of the house of Levi by itself, and their wives by themselves; the family of the Shimeites by itself, and their wives by themselves; 14 and all the families that are left, each by itself, and their wives by themselves.*

There will be a great outpouring of individual conversion. The Lord's anger will be turned away through salvation in His Son, the One whom they pierced, the One they will look upon and mourn, recognizing that they rejected the Messiah.

Zechariah 13:1 *"On that day there shall be a fountain opened for the house of David and the inhabitants of Jerusalem, to cleanse them from sin and uncleanness. 2 "And on that day, declares the LORD of hosts, I will cut off the names of the idols from the land, so that they shall be remembered no more. And also I will remove from the land the prophets and the spirit of uncleanness.*

HE WILL MAKE THEM FRUITFUL (14:5-7)

After God has saved Israel, the next thing He will do is to make them fruitful. He will be the source of their fruitfulness, *like the dew*, the one who gently waters them without destroying them, and then their fruit will appear. They will *blossom like the lily*. Their fruit will remain because they'll *take root like the trees of Lebanon*.

Jesus says much the same thing while speaking to the disciples.

John 15:16 *You did not choose me, but I chose you and appointed you that you should go and bear fruit and that your fruit should abide, so that whatever you ask the Father in my name, he may give it to you.*

Maybe Matthew heard this and thought, "Yes, You called me as I was sitting collecting taxes, but I chose to follow You. Maybe Peter could say, "I remember when I was out fishing and You came by and called me, and I chose to leave those nets and my father's business behind to follow You. I chose You." Yes, there was a human choice made, but behind the human choice, from all eternity was the choice of God that explains the choices of men. God had to grant them, and to grant us, the heart that says, "Yes."

Just as Israel was chosen and ordained for fruitfulness, He has chosen you and me and ordained that we will be fruitful.

God Will Be the Source of the Fruit (14:5)

God then gives a picture of this fruitfulness affecting others. There will be a public display of the salvation of God as their fruitfulness becomes apparent. In verse 6, He describes their *roots* spreading out and their beauty being *like the olive*. Like a *fragrance*, the world will recognize the saving work of God in this people. Israel will *return* to the land He's promised them, and they will *dwell beneath* His *shadow*. They're going to *flourish*, be fruitful *like grain*, *blossom like the vine*, and their *fame* will be like *the wine of Lebanon*. It will be a new and better day because of His tender care and provision.

The Fruit Will Appear

Israel will *blossom* or bud *like the lily*. God will cause it, though it will seem impossible. Lilies often appear rather suddenly, sprouting from what seemed like nothing.

The Fruit Will Remain

Israel will take root like the *trees of Lebanon*. God will sustain it. Lebanon was known for its cedars, mentioned about 20 times in the Bible, and also for cypress and acacia trees.

For a similar verse, see Isaiah 27:6.

The Fruit Will Have an Effect on Others (14:6)

There will be a public display of the salvation of God as their fruitfulness is apparent. Israel's *shoots will spread out*. There will be *beauty ... like the olive*. There will be *fragrance like Lebanon* with its cedars as the world will recognize the saving work of God in this people.

It Will Be a New and Better Day (14:7)

They will *return*—once again be in the land the Lord has promised them. They will be protected, living under His *shadow*. People will see that they *flourish* like *grain* and *blossom* like the grape *vine*. They will be famous, like Lebanon's *wine*.

It's wonderful to know that this is always salvation's story. The Lord has ordained that those who are saved will be fruitful.

CLOSING CHALLENGE (14:8-9)

Hosea 14 finishes with the Lord's closing challenge.

See the Choice (14:8)

In verse 8, after this whole message, the Lord basically says to the people of Israel, the people living at that time, "Look at the choice. I've set life and death before you." He asks, *what have I to do with idols?* God has nothing to do with idols, so if you want God, you must set aside idols. If you choose the way of idols, you choose the way of death, a transitory pathway that ends with nothing.

There are many so-called gods, but the Lord reminds them—and us— of His uniqueness: *It is I who answer* (hear prayers and respond) *and look after you.* Unlike the Baals, and unlike all of the other things that people give their whole lives to today, He is alive and personal.

Not only is the Lord the source of fruitfulness, as we've seen. He's also the source of everlasting life. He says, *I am like an evergreen cypress; from me comes your fruit.* So, there will be everlasting fruitfulness, everlasting gain, everlasting life: this is the Lord.

Take Action (14:9

Finally, in verse 9, God is urging Israel to act. Making a choice is not passive; it requires action.

Understand and Know

His call for the *wise* to *understand* and for the *discerning* to *know* reminds us of our Savior saying, *He who has ears to hear, let him hear.* What do you need to do with Hosea's message? Understand it. Know it. That is, believe it, that *the ways of the LORD are right*. Then act on it. *The upright walk in* His ways.

Or Stumble

If they don't walk in the Lord's ways, they will be transgressors who *stumble in them*. There's no room for something halfway. There's no room for a partial belief that tries to serve both the Lord and the idols. There's no room for only following the parts of the Lord's plan that we want. The story, probably apocryphal, is told of a soldier under Alexander the Great. The soldier tried to flee and was caught. He ended up at the feet of Alexander the Great, who asked him, "What is your name?" The soldier replied, "Alexander." He then was told, "Change your name or change your ways." If you call yourself "Christian" but your ways deny your profession, change your name or change your ways.

CONCLUSION TO THE BOOK

God has used Hosea to communicate His anger toward Israel. They have forsaken Him, their one and true God, for idols they have made with their own hands. He warns them and describes their judgment. Then, after all the warnings, God still offers them salvation, if they will return to Him. He still loves them and promises that in the future He will heal their apostasy. He will forgive them, restore their land and restore their fruitfulness.

Like Israel, we must decide how to respond to His message. If you believe it, take up your cross and follow the Son of God into His paths of fruitfulness. Then one day, when the road is finished and you stand in His presence, you'll understand that the salvation story is not about you, but about Him. What a good, merciful and gracious God He is!

22
Study Guide

LESSON 1 – A LIVING SERMON – 1:1-2:1

Reading to Prepare:
  Read Hosea 1-3 in one sitting.

  1. Why are the minor prophets called "minor"?
  2. What three possible explanations have been given for what Hosea did concerning Gomer?
  3. If you had been Hosea, what would you have been thinking and feeling?
  4. What is the spiritual significance of the Lord's command to Hosea?
  5. Explain the name of Gomer's first child, a son.
  6. Explain the name of Gomer's second child, a daughter.
  7. Explain the name of Gomer's third child, another son.
  8. How would you compare your assignment from God to Hosea's?
  9. What does being the Lord's servant mean in your life?
  10. If your life is to be a living letter, what will that mean? How will it affect your behavior and your attitudes?

LESSON 2 – LOVING JUDGMENT – 2:2-13

Reading to Prepare:
  Read Hosea 2.
  Isaiah 50:1; 54:5-8
  Ezekiel 16:35-41

  1. Can a rebuke or a stern warning be an act of love? Why or why not?

2. How does national loyalty mix with calling a nation to repentance?

3. In what sense is it true that God and Israel are like a man and his estranged wife? In what sense is it also true that the Lord has not fully divorced Israel?

4. What's the difference between being sorry for sins and repenting of sins? How can we tell the difference?

5. How is the future nakedness of Israel like the nakedness of her spiritual immorality? (What will it be like if all of your sin is exposed?)

6. Notice each main topic under "God's Judgments Determined." Without gossiping, have you seen these troubles result from sins—whether of an individual or of a nation?

7. Where do you find your main sense of satisfaction, your chief love? (How would your family or your closest friends answer this question about you?)

8. When you look at the good things in your life, do you more often credit yourself, or God? Does your confidence for the future come from your bank account? Your credentials and reputation? Your family? Your horoscope? Or from God's promises to care for you?

9. Do you realize that everything you are and have belongs to the Lord, and then use it all for Him?

10. If you sin, do you have appropriate shame and real repentance?

11. Are you experiencing God's hand of discipline right now? If so, what would He have you do about it?

LESSON 3 – WOUNDING TO HEAL – 2:14-23

Reading to Prepare:
   Read Hosea 2.
   Joshua 7
   Ezekiel 16:35-41
   Isaiah 11:6-9

1. When you were a child, did a doctor ever have to wound you to heal you? If so, did you understand?

2. How would you describe the mood of Hosea 2:14-23? What kind of music might go along with it?

3. Are the Lord's fierceness and His tenderness equally real to you?

4. Explain the background of the Valley of Achor.

5. How or why will that valley be a door of hope?

6. Have you experienced renewed faithfulness to the Lord in your life? In another's life? Who produces that?

7. When will Israel be totally dedicated to the Lord?

8. What kind of changes are described in terms of the weather, the land, and the crops? To what extent is good or bad weather the result of the Lord's response to our actions?
9. How is it possible for God to use judgment to bring salvation?
10. How can devastation be the place where beauty is born?

LESSON 4 – A STORY OF LOVE AND REDEMPTION – 3:1-5

Reading to Prepare:
Read Hosea 3.
Romans 9-11

1. People who are newly in love often say that they can't even express how great it is. Do you ever feel that way about what God has given in Christ Jesus? Why or why not?
2. What does the Lord command Hosea to do?
3. How is Gomer's character like Israel's?
4. Why would it be hard for Hosea to do this?
5. Have you ever considered the idea that love can be chosen? Why would a chosen love be superior to a love based on the lovability of the one who's loved?
6. How can we love for a higher cause?
7. What part does forgiveness play in lasting love?
8. How is Gomer's situation like ours?
9. What do you suppose Hosea's friends thought of his actions in buying Gomer at the slave market in order to have her again as his wife? What do you suppose she felt?
10. What changes must there be in Gomer's life? In Israel's? In ours?
11. What do God's love for Israel, Hosea's love for Gomer, and Christ's love for the church have in common? How does that impact your view of love and marriage?

LESSON 5 – GOD'S CONTROVERSY WITH HIS PEOPLE, PART 1 – 4:1-3

Reading to Prepare:
Read Hosea 4.
Psalm 36:1-4
Romans 1:28-32
Deuteronomy 29:18-29

1. Re-read this lesson's introduction about the portrait of a wicked person. How does that compare to Israel in Hosea's day? How

does it compare to the entertainment industry? How does it compare to your own heart and life?

2. Do you often think of sin as including what's missing that shouldn't be?

3. How does faithfulness to people relate to faithfulness to God?

4. How can a person show the kind of love that doesn't move away even in the face of mistreatment?

5. What would be some signs that the knowledge of God is missing? Or that someone is trying to replace it with mere offerings and sacrifices?

6. How do their sins relate to the ten commandments? Do you think people who continually violate several of the commandments usually think of themselves as doing so? If not, what's that say to us about sin in the human heart? (See Jeremiah 17:9-10).

7. Explain how degradation can be a part of God's judgment.

8. Have you ever considered that God's judgment may be felt in the environment?

9. How can one spiritually adulterous person be a danger to those around?

10. Have you been blaming someone else for a situation where you should be acknowledging that the problem is between you and the Lord? What are some modern examples of trying to find horizontal answers to vertical problems?

11. Look up and read the references mentioned concerning the accountability of those entrusted with leadership: Heb. 13:17; Josh. 24:15; Eph 6:4; Prov. 31:4-5.

12. How is it that people often get the leaders they deserve? Are there exceptions (good or bad) to this?

LESSON 6 – GOD'S CONTROVERSY WITH HIS PEOPLE, PART 2 – 4:4-19

Reading to Prepare:
    Read Hosea 4.
    Jude 24
    1 Kings 12:26-31
    Proverbs 6:27-29

1. Do you find it comforting or terrifying to remember that all leaders will be evaluated by the Lord?

2. How are Hosea 4:4-5 and Jude 24 opposites?

3. Have you ever rejected responsibility or wasted influence, resulting in rejected opportunity or lost influence?

4. What are some examples today of feeding on sin? What are some sins that you are tempted to feed on? Are there any sins that you need to cut off and abandon immediately?
5. Why are sorcery and false worship foolish?
6. What power or powers is/are behind the occult and behind the worship of other gods?
7. Why do people spend money, time and effort on false gods and false worship?
8. What's the connection between false worship and sexual immorality?
9. The Lord shamed Israel by telling Judah to avoid Israel. Would the Lord recommend that people hang around with you? Are you an obedient child, or like a stubborn heifer?
10. Read through and ponder or discuss the list of questions that are near the end of this lesson.

LESSON 7 – GOD'S CHARACTER AND JUDGMENT – 5:1-15

Reading to Prepare:
  Read Hosea 5.
  Romans 8:28-32
  2 Peter 2:7-9
  Amos 5:18-24

1. Do you desire the Day of the Lord? Will Jesus' return and the Day of the Lord bring you gain or loss? (Read Titus 2:13; Romans 2:5,16.)
2. God's justice is blind in the sense of being impartial. How is that good news?
3. What does the Lord see concerning Israel in Hosea's time? And what does He see concerning your nation in your time?
4. Explain the idea of God's immanence. Look up a definition of the word, if needed, and don't confuse it with *eminence* or *imminence*.
5. Explain the idea of God's transcendence.
6. Does your view of God include the idea that knowing Him is a mercy from Him? Or do you presume that men will find God whenever they wish?
7. In 5:10, what have the princes of Judah done wrong? Why does that call for God's wrath like a flood?
8. Whose fault is it that Ephraim (the northern kingdom) is oppressed?
9. How are a moth and dry rot alike? Why is it sometimes appropriate for God to remove blessings from people?

10. Do you know what it's like to have an incurable disease? (See 5:13.)
11. How is the Lord like a lion?
12. What attitudes and actions are required if people are to return to the Lord? How does the Lord offer hope in 5:15?

LESSON 8 – REPENTANCE THAT BRINGS HOPE – 6:1-3

Reading to Prepare:
Read Hosea 5:14 through chapter 6.
Zechariah 12:10
Psalm 51:4
Ezekiel 18:23, 32

1. Have you thought about the eternal nature of God's promises to Israel?
2. Have you truly recognized your responsibility for your sins? What's the difference between that and an apology that begins, "I'm sorry if anyone was offended by what I did..."?
3. When was the last time you came in repentance to God, acknowledging that He was right to confront you, and right to condemn your sin?
4. What could be some signs that God is judging us?
5. What might be some ways of distinguishing between God's judgment of sinners and God's proving of the righteous? In other words, when your world falls apart, what are some ways to know which message the Lord is sending you?
6. In what sense is every sin a sin against the Lord? How does that help us understand God's justice when He judges?
7. How can God be fierce with justice and tender with mercy at the same time?
8. What are some of the excuses that a deceptive heart may use as reasons for not repenting and for not accepting God's forgiveness? (Have you used any excuses like these?)
9. What evidence can you think of that indicates the Lord's purpose concerning Israel?
10. What's God's first desire (His pleasure) concerning sinners? What does He want from them?
11. Have you "kissed the Son"?

LESSON 9 – WHAT GOD DELIGHTS IN – 6:4-11

Reading to Prepare:
  Read Hosea 6.
  Exodus 20:7

1. Is the idea of delighting God new to you? How does the idea im-
    pact your view of your relationship with Him?
2. According to verse 6, what things explain how it's possible to take
    the Lord's name in vain through our actions?
3. Why do true love and loyalty toward people flow from our unself-
    ish commitment to God?
4. Why does loyalty to a relative sometimes require that you stand
    against what they are saying or doing?
5. How has the people's love for the Lord been like dew?
6. Explain how God's love and His faithful nature result in His warn-
    ings and His confrontation of people.
7. Can you think of an example when someone corrected you in a
    way that was humble, loving, but unmistakable?
8. What does God desire (verse 6)? What can you do in order to
    please Him, in order to give Him what he desires?
9. Ponder or discuss the questions at the end of this lesson.

LESSON 10 – WHAT GOD HATES – 6:4-11

Reading to Prepare:
  Read Hosea 6.
  Genesis 1
  1 Kings 12:25-33
  Job 1:9-11
  Isaiah 24:5

1. Are you more accustomed to thinking of God's will in terms of do-
    ing what He loves, or not doing what He hates? (Consider spend-
    ing extra time pondering the other.)
2. Are you fulfilling your promises to God? To people?
3. Re-read the list of the things God gave Adam. How do those com-
    pare with the blessings He gives those who are in Christ?
4. Have you seen lives (maybe your own) similar to the pattern that
    God's people followed in the Old Testament?
5. Are you currently doing things to people that the Lord considers
    crimes against them?

6. The people of Gilead are described as workers or makers of wickedness. Do you think of any whole industries that are, at root, makers of wickedness? To what extent, if any, are you participating or approving of this?
7. The priests described are illegitimate agents (not selected according to God's plan) of illegitimate worship (not at the places which God designated) who are planning crimes. Are you ever tempted to use religion as a cover for evil?
8. What relationship is there between false religion and immorality and defilement?
9. How can you plan for a harvest of joy instead of a harvest of judgment? (And how does Jesus relate to this?)

LESSON 11 – LIFE ON THE BRINK – 7:1-16

Reading to Prepare:
　　Read Hosea 7.
　　Revelation 2:20-23
　　Luke 23:8-12
　　Isaiah 59:1-7

1. As you have been going through this study of Hosea, have you found reasons to think that you may be headed to spiritual disaster? Or reasons to thank God that He's changed your heart? Neither? Both?
2. How does sound judgment relate to God's grace?
3. What responsibilities do you have as a result of having received God's goodness? Maybe there are more than you can name. If so, what responsibility is He pressing on you right now?
4. Read through the list of sins in Hosea 7:1-4. Is one of them more of a temptation for you than the others?
5. Have you ever thought of your sin (or your unfaithfulness, your idolatry) as being like a fire burning within you? What does that image say to you?
6. How do selfish, godless desires work against civil peace? (You may want to compare James 4:1-12.)
7. The king's associates would burn with evil plots against him. Are you plotting against anyone?
8. How is a spiritually compromised person like a half-baked cake that's overdone on the bottom and raw on top? What does it mean today for someone to be separate from worldliness and sin?
9. Do you see pride as your strength, or as your weakness? What should we teach children about pride?

10. How can sin result in impaired judgment?
11. In what way could sin impair a nation's foreign policy? Do you recall any examples of this?
12. How does sin impair judgment? Has it impaired yours? (How would you know?)

LESSON 12 – SOWING WIND, REAPING WHIRLWIND – 8:1-14

Reading to Prepare:
Read Hosea 8.
Luke 6:46
James 4:13-16
Exodus 32:1-14

1. In what way are warnings acts of grace?
2. Have you seen someone "sow the wind" (that is, sin in a seemingly small way) and "reap the whirlwind" (that is, get disastrous results)? Why doesn't that always happen?
3. How is it that sin leads to lack of "grain in the head"?
4. Think back on one or two of the worst things you've ever done to other people. Does your thought about those actions change when you realize that all sins against people are also sins against God?
5. Consider one of the smallest things you've done wrong lately, when you didn't fully, immediately trust the Lord. If you think of it as a personal transgression against Him, does that change your perspective?
6. Have you submitted not only your words and actions, but also your thoughts and feelings, to the Word of God? Or could the Lord still say of you, "They have rebelled against My law"?
7. In what way could we say that Israel's prayers were empty? (See 8:2-3.) What do you think will be the Lord's reaction to people and churches today who "spurn the good"?
8. What does it mean to be presumptuous in our choices? How does faith in the Lord interconnect with your own choices?
9. Does your life bear the marks of someone who is rebelling against God?

LESSON 13 – ABANDONED BY GOD – 9:1-9

Reading to Prepare:
Read Hosea 9.
2 Timothy 4:9-15
1 Kings 18
Hebrews 12:6

1. When Hosea says, "You have loved a prostitute's wages," what does that mean?
2. Why is it justice for the Lord to take away their blessings?
3. What blessings will be taken away?
4. What signs, if any, do you see that may indicate the withdrawal of the Lord's blessing on your nation? (What will be most people's re-action if you suggest this explanation?)
5. How does God enable us to remain sensitive to Him? Have you considered that a diminished sensitivity to God and to His Word can be a sign of His withdrawal?
6. Should we expect plots today against those who proclaim God's truth? In what way is a very secular society God's judgment on that society?
7. Has God been striving with you? That is, are you a student of His school of grace? If so, have you been welcoming His correction?
8. Do you want God to leave you alone? Or will you yield to Him?
9. The presence of God's word means hope. Will you heed it?

LESSON 14 – WHEN GOD TAKES YOUR GLORY AWAY – 9:10-17

Reading to Prepare:
Read Hosea 9.
Deuteronomy 8:11-20
Numbers 25:1-9
1 Corinthians 10:1-14
Deuteronomy 32:4-18

1. Without gossiping, can you give one or more examples of people forgetting the Lord?
2. "Only God has inherent glory." What does this mean?
3. Explain what happened at Baal-peor. Who suggested the tempta-tion? What were the results?
4. Why were the actions at Baal-peor detestable?
5. What are some things that your nation loves, but that God detests? (Do you detest what God detests?)

6. How does a person become detestable? If you or someone you know is on the path to becoming detestable, what should you do?

7. One of the ways the Lord disciplines is by removing glory. If God's glory departs from a person, a church or a community, what would be some indications of that?

8. As a Christian, is your view of children different from the world's view of them? How?

9. Israel had amazing privileges and was wasting them. What are some of the privileges that the Lord has given you? How are you using them?

10. Have you ever considered the possibility of God hating people? We are able to say that God is love, and at the same time we can believe Hosea 9:15. How do those fit together? Can you hate people for their sin, while loving them as created in God's image? (See Psalm 139:21,22.)

11. How do you look at people who have come from a Christian background, who then have outstanding worldly success, but who abandon the true God? Do you believe that God will reject them (9:17)? What will their end be? (See also Psalm 73 and Mark 8:36.)

LESSON 15 – JUDGED BY PROSPERITY – 10:1-10

Reading to Prepare:
    Read Hosea 10.
    Proverbs 27:21
    Proverbs 30:7-9
    Matthew 6:19-34
    Deuteronomy 12:1-5

1. Do you currently feel like you're in a time of prosperity with the wind at your back, or like you are struggling to barely hang on? Or is it somewhere in between?

2. In what way is your current situation a test?

3. Consider the first two questions again, but in view of your church or your nation instead of just yourself.

4. What do you treasure most? That is, what do you dream of doing or having or being? What are your most passionate thoughts? And what's that say about your heart?

5. Have you seen people put their trust in wicked rulers? (Is this different from trusting God to work through wicked rulers?)

6. Are churches tempted to make their worship like that of pagans? If so, how?

7. Have you ever substituted something else for the true God? What kinds of things have you been tempted to substitute?
8. Explain Israel's double iniquity (double sin). How could a person or a church or a nation be guilty of such double iniquity today?
9. Is your nation, on the whole, following the Lord truly, or trying to mix the Lord with idolatry, or totally rejecting Him? What will be the expected result?
10. Consider or discuss the following statements. "I want to be responsive to God's voice, so I don't have to feel His rod. I want to respond to His Word, so He won't have to take away from me things that I would substitute for Him."

LESSON 16 – SOWING AND REAPING – 10:11-15

Reading to Prepare:
    Read Hosea 10.
    Deuteronomy 30:19-20
    Genesis 2:15-18
    Jeremiah 28:12-17
    Proverbs 11:18
    Galatians 6:7-8

1. Have you ever been a gardener or a farmer? If so, what did you learn about planting and harvesting?
2. What is repentance?
3. Do you usually think of repentance as being more a gift from God, or a choice?
4. How is it that sin is both the broad way that most people choose (Matthew 7:13) and a hard way?
5. Explain plowing, harrowing, and threshing.
6. How can responsibility be a blessing?
7. Have you ever done "hard plowing" after sinning?
8. What things is Israel told to do in verse 12? What will be the results if they do them?
9. How are the Lord's warnings a blessing?
10. How do you suppose they felt when hearing the warning of verse 13?
11. Would any of the warnings of this passage apply to you? To your church? Your business? Your nation? If so, what will you do about it?

LESSON 17 – THE MOST OVERLOOKED ASPECT OF SIN – 11:1-11

Reading to Prepare:
>Read Hosea 11.
>Psalm 35:4-18
>Proverbs 17:13
>Deuteronomy 7:6-8

1. How has the Lord's care for Israel been like that of a loving earthly father?
2. How has the Lord's care for you been like that of a loving earthly father?
3. *The more they were called, the more they went away.* Does that describe your relationship to God?
4. In verses 5-7, what will Israel lose?
5. How do you see your sin? Before continuing to the next questions, try to put into words how you usually see it.
6. Do you see your sin as a personal act toward God? (How would you react to someone under your protection and authority who treated you the way you treat God?)
7. Do you see your sin as something clearly defined and identified by God's Word? Or do you make excuses for yourself day after day, year after year?
8. Do you see your sin as an act of betrayal? In what way is sin an act of betrayal?
9. Do you believe God's promises to Israel still hold?
10. How can the promised regathering of Israel (verses 10-11) be an encouragement to Jews? And how can it encourage Gentile believers in Jesus?

LESSON 18 – LEARN FROM YOUR PAST - 11:12-12:14

Read Hosea 11 and 12.
Genesis 35:1-14

1. If you're a parent, does that experience help you understand why the Lord sometimes repeats the same instructions and warnings?
2. Do you learn from the Lord's warnings?
3. Will you benefit by example and instruction? What examples has the Lord put before you of godliness, or of the disaster that's the fruit of sin, or of strong discipline in your own life?
4. Do you, like Jacob, strongly desire the blessing and favor of God?

5. Sin can be thought of in many ways, such as missing the mark, rebellion, a flaw, being trapped, and so on. When you think about sin, how do you usually think of it? In what sense is every sin an attack on God? In what sense is it grasping for wind?

6. Have you yet learned what Jacob learned? Ponder or discuss each of the following three thoughts.
    a. You don't find true blessing by falsehood and sin.
    b. You don't find true blessing without brokenness.
    c. You don't find true blessing until you arrive at submission.

7. The commentary listed five steps of repentance, based on verse 6. Review them. Is there any one of them that's harder for you than the others? If so, what will you do about it? (Does the quote, "Sin is what you do when you are not satisfied with God," help you?)

8. What is the difference between what the apostle Paul said, "I am all things to all men, that by all means I may win some," and being taken in by the worldly culture around you? Can you think of an example of something that you always assumed was good and normal, until the Lord showed you that you should not participate in it?

9. How can you keep your conscience sensitive to the Lord's will, instead of having it hardened and seared?

10. What's the difference between giving the Lord religion, and giving Him your life? In what area of your life is He asking you to trust Him fully, more fully than at present? Will you do it?

11. Has the Lord removed your bloodguilt (12:14), or will He repay you for your disgraceful deeds? What do you need to say to Him?

LESSON 19 – THE AUTOPSY OF A NATION – 13:1-16

Reading to Prepare:
Read Hosea 13.
Genesis 48:1-20
Jeremiah 2:26-28
Revelation 6:15-17
Revelation 14:9-13

1. How would you feel if you lived in an outwardly prosperous nation, but if you were almost sure it was heading toward disaster?

2. In Genesis 3, what's the original cause of death in the world?

3. What's the difference between spiritual death and physical death? How can a person or a nation be alive in one sense, but dead in a deeper sense?

4. Which of the 12 tribes of Israel was considered most powerful?

5. What are the results of idolatry? How may those be seen today?
6. What do mist, dew, chaff and smoke picture in this chapter?
7. What indicates that they rejected God's self-revelation? What today would be some indicators of that sort of rejection by a person or by a nation?
8. How is it that the Lord is both their helper and their enemy? (And who is to blame for that?)
9. When God mocks, do you think it is with a smug "I told you so" attitude, or is it to point out the foolishness of worshiping any other god?
10. Compare Hosea 13:14 and 1 Corinthians 15:55. Note how Hosea and the apostle Paul use the words differently as the two men speak of different people.
11. When you think of standing in the presence of the Lord, what do you feel? If something other than terror, what is the basis for your confidence? (Is it because of something you've done, or something He's done?)

LESSON 20 – COMING HOME – 14:1-3

Reading to Prepare:
   Read Hosea 14.
   Luke 15
   Psalm 51

1. What is the main message of the book of Hosea? Is that message popular today?
2. What's the main message of these three verses?
3. Is repentance a word that you've used in conversation in the past few months? Why or why not?
4. What's the difference between self-improvement and repentance?
5. How is repentance personal? Have you thought of it that way before?
6. What's the difference between repentance and regret?
7. Have you usually thought of repenting as something that your conscience and your church, your family, and your peers call you to, or as something that the Lord calls you to? What difference does it make?
8. When you read in Luke 15 about the prodigal son and the waiting Father, which of the two sons is more like you?
9. What things are you tempted to depend on instead of the Lord? Are you willing to turn completely from trusting them?
10. If you repent and ask the Lord's mercy, what will He do for you?

LESSON 21 – ISRAEL'S SALVATION AND OURS – 14:4-9

Reading to Prepare:
>   Read Hosea 14.
>   Romans 2:5
>   Romans 11:25-36
>   Jeremiah 13:23
>   Ezekiel 36:22-38

1. How do man's responsibility to be holy, man's inability to be holy, and God's provision for us intersect? How do they relate to each other?
2. If we're commanded to repent, how can we say that repentance is a gift from God? Does He force us to repent against our will?
3. What are some of the reasons people give as to why God loves them? What is the clear reason? (Do you ever find it odd that God could love someone like you?)
4. What do we mean when we say, "God has been propitiated toward them?"
5. How would most people describe a fruitful life? How would God describe it?
6. Where does lasting fruit come from?
7. What's the effect of the fruit the Lord gives? (Have you ever seen the Lord give a person or a ministry vastly expanded fruitfulness, far beyond what would have seemed likely?)
8. The Lord urged the people to understand and to know. How can we read or hear the scriptures in such a way that we understand and know? Do you have any tips concerning that?
9. Why is repentance essential?
10. What do you most want to remember about this study of the book of Hosea?

www.ingramcontent.com/pod-product-compliance
Lightning Source LLC
La Vergne TN
LVHW051235080426
835513LV00016B/1608